SON OF GOD
SON OF THE SUN

THE LIFE AND PHILOSOPHY OF AKHENATEN, KING OF EGYPT

D1706796

Creative Fire Press
2015

SON OF GOD
SON OF THE SUN

THE LIFE AND PHILOSOPHY OF AKHENATEN, KING OF EGYPT

BY

SAVITRI DEVI

Creative Fire Press
2015

Editor: David Skrbina.

Library of Congress Cataloging-in-Publication Data

Savitri Devi
Son of God, Son of the Sun: The Life and Philosophy of Akhenaten, King of Egypt

     p.   cm.
Includes bibliographical references.

ISBN 978-069-237194-7 (pbk.: alk. paper)
   1. Philosophy. 2. History, ancient Egypt.
   2015

Printing number: 9 8 7 6 5 4 3 2 1

Printed in the United States of America on acid-free paper.

DEDICATION

To my husband. – SD

To all those future disciples of light. – DS

ACKNOWLEDGMENT

The present text was derived from the 1946 edition of Savitri's book *A Son of God* (Calcutta: Savitri Devi Mukherji). Subsequent editions were published under the title *Son of the Sun*. File source was the Savitri Devi Archive (www.savitridevi.org).

The editor wishes to acknowledge the efforts of Dr. R. G. Fowler and Gabriella at the Archive. Their work has been indispensible for the preservation and promotion of Savitri's publications.

— DS

CONTENTS

SON OF GOD
SON OF THE SUN

THE LIFE AND PHILOSOPHY
OF AKHENATEN,
KING OF EGYPT

EDITOR'S PREFACE

DAVID SKRBINA

Think of Western civilization as a grand mansion. It houses a vast array of human genius: *Hamlet* and the Sistine Chapel, the 9th Symphony and the Mona Lisa, gothic cathedrals and the microcomputer. It is a structure with many great pillars, including music, art, science, literature, technology. These pillars rest on two foundation stones: Christian theology, and ancient Greek culture and philosophy. But these two core elements of Western civilization are not suspended in thin air; they rest in turn on a deeper and firmer bedrock. And that bedrock is ancient Egypt.

The culture of ancient Egypt is surely the least well-understood aspect of our entire modern existence—even as it is the ultimate basis for all we think and know. The conflict between monism and dualism, the concept of the soul, the nature of the afterlife, basic moral precepts, ideas about nature: all these ideas were founded at that time. Beginning some 5,000 years ago, circa 3200 BC, a cohesive Egyptian society emerged from disparate desert tribes of the Nile delta. Until their defeat by Alexander the Great in 332 BC, the Egyptians sustained the longest continuous civilization in human history—running nearly 3,000 years. Over these three millennia, Egyptians constructed the foundation of what would become our own civilization.

Owing to its antiquity, much of the empire's accomplishments have been lost; but as well, much remains. The Great Pyramids at Giza and the Sphinx were built around 2550 BC, during what we now call the Old Kingdom. We have many works of pottery, carvings, artwork, and inscriptions dating from that time. Among these items are the pyramid texts of 2350 BC—perhaps the oldest human writings that we possess. We also know bits and pieces of the many kings and pharaohs that came to power—their lives, their accomplishments, and their downfall. It was during this vast span of time that the key elements of Western mythology, religion, and philosophy came into being. Bear in mind: Egyptian culture was already some 2,600 years old *before* the first Greek philosopher ever saw the light of day.

Of the roughly 275 Egyptian rulers that we know by name, perhaps the most significant, and surely the most fascinating, is the young pharaoh Akhenaten. During his short life and span of rule, he articulated a worldview and philosophy of profound importance. According to one recent commentator, Akhenaten devised nothing less than a "religion of light."[1] In truth, though, his vision was less a religion and more of a comprehensive metaphysical worldview; it was, as we shall see, a *metaphysics of light.*

«««—»»»

A few basic facts of his life are in order. As was common in that day, Akhenaten was truly a 'boy king.' Assuming power at age 13, he reigned for only 17 years, until his death at age 29. But this short time was sufficient to distill the wisdom of ages past, and to articulate a philosophical system of unprecedented beauty and depth.

The details are hazy, but we are now able to piece together the key events of his life. Akhenaten was born around 1365 BC to the pharaoh Amenhotep III and Queen Tiye.[2] His birth name was Amenhotep IV, and he was widely known as Prince Amenhotep; the change to 'Akhenaten' came later in life. He was born during a period that we now refer to as the New Kingdom, a time of unequaled wealth and power for the Egyptian empire. As the second of two sons, we might not have heard anything at all from the young prince, except that his older brother Thutmose died before he could assume power—leaving Akhenaten as the sole male heir.

Amenhotep III passed away in or about the year 1353, thus making Akhenaten supreme ruler of Egypt at age 13. As was custom at that time, he took a young bride: a slightly older and strikingly beautiful girl by the name of Nefertiti. In one of many ironies in this story, she has eclipsed her illustrious husband in popular culture, becoming the second most well-known queen of ancient Egypt—after Cleopatra.[3] Akhenaten and Nefertiti had children at a surprisingly early age. Their first daughter, Merit-aten, was born already in his first year of reign. Two more royal daughters followed in the next few years: Meket-aten and Ankhesenpa-aten. Ultimately they would have six girls.

---

[1] Hornung (1995).

[2] To add to our confusion of this era are trivial matters such as the spelling of places and names. Amenhotep is sometimes referred to by the Greek spelling 'Amenophis.' Tiye is occasionally written 'Tiy.' The names of the gods vary: 'Amun' and 'Amon,' for example, and 'Ra' or 'Re.' Even Akhenaten's name has seen many variations: Akhenaton, Akhnaton, Echnaton, etc. The difficulty arises, in large part, from transcribing hieroglyphics into English or Latin equivalents.

[3] There were in fact many 'Cleopatras' in antiquity. 'The' Cleopatra is more accurately known as Cleopatra VII Philopater, who lived from roughly 69 to 30 BC.

In his sixth regnal year, at age 18, Akhenaten founded a new city to be his capital; he named it Akhet-aten, or 'Horizon of the Aten'.[4] As we will see, 'Aten' was the ancient name for the sun—specifically, for the solar disk itself (the Egyptians having, of course, no real concept of the sun as a distant ball of fire.) The city of Akhet-aten was to be the figurative seat of Aten—the sole and true god of the cosmos, in Akhenaten's view. The Aten became, during his rule, the focal point around which everything revolved. Akhenaten's own name, which he gave to himself in his fifth regnal year, means something like 'Effective for the Aten' or 'He who is useful to the Aten' or 'Glorified spirit of the Aten.'

Akhenaten's emphasis on Aten, the sun, was in itself not original. The concept and name of the solar disk was already quite old, dating back at least to the Twelfth Dynasty, circa 1900 BC. The sun had long been a member of the Egyptian pantheon, which included such notable deities as Amun (creator god), Atum (creator and sun god), Geb (earth god), Horus (god of sky, sun, war), Isis (funerary, motherhood, magic), Maat (truth, justice, order), Osiris (death and resurrection), Ptah (creator), Ra/Re (sun), and Thoth (wisdom).[5] Depending on local tradition, the sun was known variously as Aten, Re (or Ra), Amun-Re, Re-Horakhty, and so on. It was long recognized as the giver of life, and as a potent force of nature.

Akhenaten's vision, however, went far beyond the sun as a natural power. His originality came in many ways: his thorough-going monism, his metaphysical vision, his integration of nature, and his intellectual and emotional connection to the sun, among others. But his most profound insight was that the sun was not a person, not a deity in the traditional sense, not even a 'thing'; rather, the divinity of the sun lay precisely and explicitly in its *light*. It was the *light of the sun*—its divine and life-giving rays, its creative energy, its sustenance of the Earth—that was the one true reality. The light is the One, and "the One is the source of cosmic existence."[6]

For Akhenaten, all things are created and infused by this divine light, which is embodied in the heat and light of the sun. In short, for Akhenaten, *all is light*. Even to the present day, some 3,300 years later, we have scarcely begun to comprehend the significance of this insight.

This metaphysical vision—'all is light'—consumed his life. Affairs of state became insignificant. Border disputes were hardly worth his time. Financial matters, priestly squabbles, and international relations faded into trivialities. All

---

[4] In more modern times the city was known as Amarna (or more formally, Tell el-Amarna) and hence we frequently see this name still used. The art of Akhenaten's day is "Amarna-style"; his correspondences are "the Amarna letters"; and so on.

[5] The Egyptians had well over 100 gods in their cosmology.

[6] Assmann (1997: 188).

that mattered for Akhenaten was to reconstruct society around the image and symbol of the Aten as the one true source of everything. His new city of Akhet-aten, his family life, his artwork, and his writings all reflected this emphasis on the Light. Metaphysics flourished, even as affairs of state suffered.

As mentioned, the royal couple eventually had six daughters. They were clearly a joy to the pharaoh, but the monarchy called for a male heir. With pre-sumably growing frustration, Akhenaten, following royal tradition, took as a consort his own sister. We do not know her name; archaeologists refer to her simply as "the younger lady."[7] But she clearly was not a 'wife' in any tradi-tional sense. No reliefs mention her, no hymns were written to her, no images survive. Akhenaten's true spouse was and always would be Nefertiti. His sister, and other possible consorts, existed strictly for the sake of necessity. In any case, the union with his sister was a success. He fathered a boy, given the name Tutankh-aten, or 'Living image of the Aten.' Today we know this child as Tutankhamen, or King Tut—the most famous boy-king in history.

In the 16th regnal year, for unknown reasons, Nefertiti died. She was barely 30 years of age. Akhenaten was soon to follow; he died the next year at the age of 29. Again, the reasons for his death are obscure. Some have pos-tulated a hunting or chariot accident. Others suggest the plague or malaria. Some point to inherited genetic abnormalities, common to royal inbreeding. The author of the present book, Savitri Devi, has suggested that he was per-haps poisoned by a jealous and vengeful priesthood—one that surely despised his monotheism of the Aten and subsequent abandonment of all other tradi-tional gods.

Akhenaten's apparent corpse was discovered in 1907 by Edward Ayrton and Arthur Weigall, in a tomb designated as KV55. The coffin, inscribed with Atenist phrasing, was evidently originally intended for a woman—but the body was shown to be a male, and of the appropriate age at death to be Akhenaten. For decades, experts were of divided opinion on the identity of the mummy. Recently, in 2010, advanced DNA testing was performed on the body.[8] The individual was shown to be both the son of Amenhotep III and the father of Tutankhamen—and hence Akhenaten. The skeleton resides today in the Cairo Museum.

Following Akhenaten's death, there was a two-year period of turmoil. An obscure figure, Smenkhkare, seems to have come to rule the empire. But he (or she) quickly vanished, to be replaced by the new boy-king, Tutankhamen. King Tut assumed power at the strikingly young age of 8, ruling for just 10 years. We know him, of course, not so much for his accomplishments as his

---

[7] Her mummified body was discovered in 1898, but only recently identified through DNA testing.

[8] Hawass, et al. (2010).

gorgeously intact burial chamber and coffin, which were discovered in 1922. In a final connection to his father, it appears that Tut took as 'brides' two of his own older half-sisters, Meritaten and Anhkhesenpaaten. The former died early in Tut's reign; the latter, just two years after it ended.

By the year 1320 BC, then, Akhenaten and his family line had vanished from the earth. The philosophy of light was gone, hidden away but not lost—to sleep for more than three millennia. Today it reawakens, in a new splendor and with a new urgency.

«« —»»

All periods of Egyptian history are distinguished by their artwork, but that of the Amarna period is particularly stunning. It is marked by one notable image, an icon of striking power and insight: the Aten, the disk of the sun, with rays beaming down, each terminating in a small hand. The hands are delicate, and compelling. Each one is slightly cupped, fingers together, thumb apart—touching but not grabbing. This image—'rays ending in hands'—shows the sun, Aten, reaching down to earth, gracing all with his power and his light. Often the hands are open, but occasionally they carry a gift, such as the *ankh*, the symbol of life. This iconography is utterly unique to Akhenaten's reign, and may even have been his own construction; it appears nowhere else, either before or after him. It is the definitive marker of the Religion of the Disk.

The sun imagery, with the rays ending in hands, gives us a pictorial concept of Akhenaten's worldview. Other clues come from scattered artworks, sculptures, and occasional relics. Regarding textual sources, hieroglyphic references are rare. In fact we have today only two short texts on the Atenist philosophy, both apparently written by the pharaoh himself. These are poems or hymns to Aten—designated as the Longer (or 'Greater') and Shorter ('Lesser') Hymns. Translating poetry from any language is difficult, but interpreting a hieroglyphic source is a truly daunting task. Many English translations exist, especially for the Longer Hymn. Here I include two versions: at the start of the book, a contemporary translation of the Longer Hymn; and at the end, one in more traditional ('thee/thou') religious terminology. Also at the end is a version of the Shorter Hymn, following Lichtheim (1973).

On the surface of it, Akhenaten's philosophy appears as little more than archaic sun-worship—scarcely different than that practiced by countless ancient societies. What makes him special? Why his significance? Why should a metaphysic of sun-worship be relevant to us today? It seems silly: We moderns know all-too-well that there is no reason to worship the sun. It rises every day, it warms us, it brings light—whether we pray to it or not. It wanes in the autumn and winter, and returns every spring, no matter our attitude toward it. Yes, it is vital to our survival—but why waste our time honoring a big ball of fire?

But consider this obvious fact: The ancients were not stupid. They knew that the sun came every day, no matter what they did. They knew that the rising sun was the virtual definition of regularity and dependability. Akhenaten did not pray to it so that it would come. He prayed to it because he was honoring it, and the Big Light that it represents, as the source of all existence. He was honoring his life, the life of his family, and that of his subjects. He was honoring nature. He was honoring all creation and the motive force of the cosmos. Ultimately he was honoring *existence itself.* A prayer to the sun is an acknowledgement of the joy of existence—the privilege of being graced by the cosmos to spend even a short time here, basking in the glorious Light that is the source of all.

Contemplating this situation brings a realization of the connectedness of all life, and all being. All life depends on the sun. All matter (we now understand) comes from the stars. All existence is endowed with sensitivity, with awareness, and with energy. In this sense, we are not unique. *We belong here. The cosmos is our home.* In a way, we, of all universal beings, are uniquely capable of absorbing this fact. And Akhenaten was perhaps the first man in history to truly grasp the meaning of this wisdom.

As this insight penetrated into the mind of the young pharaoh, it evidently brought a deep sense of calm and serenity. This wisdom demanded, furthermore, that he model his life and actions on the gentle benevolence of the rising sun. As a leader, time and again, he refused to take military action against his opponents. He refused to hunt. His offerings to Aten emphasized the non-violent bounty of bread, wine, fruits, and vegetables. His formal pictures and engravings showed placid family scenes, and loving offerings to the one god Aten. Military figures were often present—always in the background—but typical Egyptian scenes of brutality, victory, or death were all but nonexistent.

All this suggests an ultimate aim of the Religion of the Sun: to achieve an exalted state of being, one that Akhenaten calls "*Ankh-em-Maat.*" *Ankh* is life, and is symbolized by the looped cross.[9] *Maat* was, in the Old Kingdom, Goddess of Truth. In the New Kingdom of Amarna, *Maat* refers simply to the larger sense of truth, harmony, and justice that reigns in the cosmos, by its very nature. *Ankh-em-Maat*, then, means to 'live in truth'—to attune oneself to the cosmic harmony, and to achieve that internal peace of mind that marks a truly just person. *Living in Truth*—this was the aim of the Religion of the Disk.

---

[9] This, centuries before that other Cross came to represent 'life eternal.'

‹‹‹—›››

Much has been written on Akhenaten since his existence came again to light in the 1800s. From early works like Petrie's *Tell el-Amarna* (1894) and Davies' *The Rock Tombs at Amarna* (1903) to recent books by Hornung (1995) and Assmann (1997), we find the typical range of scholarly opinion. In addition to the academic material, we have today an array of popular references: novels, plays, musical treatments ranging from heavy metal and rock to jazz and opera, films, and even comic books—all drawing on the legend of the young king. As we might expect, the scholarly works are serious, analytical, and objective, whereas the popular treatments are whimsical, speculative, and heavily endowed with poetic license.

Since we are seeking here a serious look at the story of Akhenaten, we can dismiss all popular accounts. This leaves us with the academic and scholarly works of archaeologists as our standard of reference. The problem for us is that Akhenaten, though obviously an historical figure, was, in essence, a poet and a philosopher. And archaeologists, to a man, know almost nothing about poetry or philosophy. Hence they are in a poor position to assess the content and value of Akhenaten's life work.

What we need, then, is someone well-versed in poetry and philosophy, a sensitive scholar, one who will treat the subject with all due seriousness but who is still attuned to the deeper metaphysical and aesthetic issues at hand. Such a person is to be valued in any field, and is, particularly in recent times, extremely rare. Thus we are most fortunate to find such a woman as Savitri Devi, the author of our present work.

This is not the place to tell her life story—something that demands a book in itself. Suffice to say that she was, at once, a most colorful, intelligent, and controversial woman. Born Maximiani Julia Portas in Lyon, France in 1905, Savitri studied philosophy and chemistry at the university there, eventually earning a PhD in philosophy. She spent most of the 1930s and early 1940s in India, marrying the Indian historian and journalist Asit Mukherji. By the late 1940s she was back in Europe, publishing books and becoming politically active. Ideologically speaking, Savitri Devi promoted environmental awareness and animal rights at a time when neither was popular. She was a dedicated vegetarian. In terms of politics, she was a radical socialist, albeit of a nationalist orientation. From a religious standpoint, she despised Judeo-Christianity (more so the former than the latter), but found deep meaning in orthodox Hinduism. Most important of all was her devotion to the ideas and vision of the long-dead Egyptian king. Savitri died in 1982 while visiting a friend in England; she was 77.

Throughout her lifetime Savitri published several works on Akhenaten, including the pamphlet "Akhnaton's Eternal Message" (1940), *Joy of the Sun* (1942), "Akhnaton: A Play" (1948), and *The Lightning and the Sun* (1958). The most important of such works, though, was her 1946 book *A Son of God*—the subject piece at hand. Although the original version of her book is now some 70 years old, most of her information is still valid; where needed, I have corrected the facts. But more importantly, her interpretation and synthesis of ideas is as valid as ever.

From the second edition on, she changed the title to *Son of the Sun*. In the present work, I have elected to resolve this dichotomy by synthesizing the two titles. I trust that she would approve.

My objectives in editing this work are many. First and foremost, of course, is to bring Savitri's writing, and consequently Akhenaten's vision, to the attention of a new 21st century audience. To the best of my knowledge, all past editions of this book are out of print and hard to obtain. For this new edition, I have cleaned up her original text, edited down some protracted discussions, and narrowed the focus. Spellings have been standardized and updated (American standard), and factual information corrected, in order to not mislead the reader. Diagrams, artwork, and section titles have been added. Footnotes have been streamlined. The aim is to produce a concise, readable, accurate, and engaging account of Akhenaten's life. I hope I have succeeded.

Above all, however, I have attempted to preserve the grace and elegance of her writing, and to allow Akhenaten's vision to shine through. Savitri has written a beautiful book. In the end, it is nothing less than a love letter to Akhenaten. May that love grace us all.

LONGER HYMN TO ATEN

(CONTEMPORARY TRANSLATION)

(1)
As you, Aten, rise over the horizon,
Your beauty, Giver of Life, is revealed.
You rise in the east,
You fill the land with beauty.
Your glory shines high above the land,
Your rays enrich the land you have created.

O Re, you reach to the ends of the earth,
You bestow these lands on Akhenaten, your beloved son.
Although you are far away,
Your rays touch the earth.
Although you shine on every human face,
No one sees you go.

(2)
When you set upon the western horizon,
The earth lies in darkness and death.
Sleepers lie beneath their covers,
Seeing no one around them.
Their belongings under their pillows could vanish,
They would not even notice.
The lion leaves his cave,
The snake strikes,
When darkness blankets the land.
The lands are quiet,
Their creator rests on the horizon.

(3)

At daybreak, you rise again over the horizon,
You shine as the Aten bringing day.
Your rays chase away the darkness,
The Two Lands of Egypt rejoice.
Awake and erect,
You raise them up.
Bathed and dressed,
They raise their hands in praise.
The whole land goes to work.

(4)

Cattle graze contented,
Trees and plants turn green.
Birds fly to their nests,
They spread their wings to praise your soul.
All things that walk or fly come to life
When you have risen.
Ships and barges sail up and down,
Canals open at your rising.
Fish glide through the river,
Your rays penetrate even dark waters.

(5)

You join a woman and a man,
You massage the fetus in its mother's womb,
You soothe the crying child unborn,
You nurse the hungry infant in the womb,
You breathe into its nostrils the first breath of life.
You open the newborn's mouth on the day of its birth,
You meet every human need.

(6)

The chick in the egg,
Which speaks already in the shell,
You give it the breath therein to bring life.
You have set its due time
To break the shell of the egg;
It emerges from the egg
To speak at its due time;
It is already running about on its feet
When it emerges from it.

(7)
Innumerable are your unseen deeds,
You have no equal!
Alone, you fashioned the earth according to your plan,
All humans and animals, all that walk and fly.

(8)
In Syria-Palestine, Ethiopia, and Egypt,
You assign each a place.
You allot to each both needs and food,
You count out to each the days of life.
They have separate languages,
And varied natures as well.
Their skins are different,
For you have so distinguished the peoples.

(9)
You have made a Nile in the underworld,
So it may be brought forth at your command
To feed the people of the land.
Thus have you made them, wearying yourself
On their behalf, you are lord of all.
In this way the Aten of the day arises,
Majestic in its greatness.
You also give life to all distant lands,
For you have placed a Nile in the heavens,
So that rain may fall upon the sea and make waves
Upon the mountains like those in the sea, irrigating their fields.

(10)
How efficient are your designs, O lord of all time,
With this Nile for the other lands and their creatures,
With a Nile springing from the underworld for Egypt.

Your rays give sustenance to every field,
Your rising brings them life and growth.
You have established the seasons
To nurture all that you have made,
The winter to cool them and the heat,
So they may feel your touch.
You made the heavens in which to rise,
That you might observe all things.

(11)
You alone are the Aten,
Yet you alone rise.
You alone are the source of life.
Appearing, glistening, departing and reappearing,
Your manifestations are without number.
You are the Aten, the source of life.
Every village, harbor, field, road, and river sees your light,
They feel your warmth.
You are the Aten,
You are the light of the earth.

(12)
You are my desire,
No one knows you except Akhenaten, your son.
You have revealed yourself to me,
You have shown me your plans and your power.

Your hand made Egypt,
You created it.
When you rise,
The earth lives.
When you set,
The earth dies.
You are life itself,
All live through you.
Every eye sees clearly until you set,
All work must wait until you rise again.
At your rising, every arm works for your pharaoh,
At your creation, every foot sets off to work.

You raise up the people for the son of your body,
For the pharaoh of Upper and Lower Egypt.

(Closing)
Akhenaten rules with Ma'at, the divine patron of knowledge,
The son of Re, who lives on Ma'at,
The lord of diadem, Akhenaten, great in his lifetime,
And the great king's wife, whom he loves,
The mistress of the Two Lands,
Nefer-neferu-aten Nefertiti,
Who lives and is rejuvenated
Forever and ever.

— contemporary translation, based on Matthews and Benjamin (2006)

Fig. 1: Akhenaten, Nefertiti, and three of their six daughters, in familial bliss.

INTRODUCTION

Thou art in my heart;
There is no other that knoweth Thee,
Save Thy Son, Akhenaten.
Thou hast made him wise in Thy designs
And in Thy might.

Akhenaten—*Longer Hymn to the Sun*
(Translation by Breasted)

The modern world has yet adequately to value or
even to acquaint itself with this man who, in an age so
remote and under conditions so adverse, became the world's
first idealist and the world's first *individual.*

Breasted (1912: 392)

Roughly fourteen hundred years before Christ, at the time Egypt was at the height of her power, King Akhenaten ruled over that great country for a few years.

The aim of the present book is to tell the world how perfect Akhenaten was.

He was a thinker; he was an artist; he was a saint—the world's first rationalist, and the oldest Prince of Peace. Through the visible disk of the sun—the Aten—he worshipped "the Energy within the Disk": the ultimate reality which men of all creeds still seek, knowingly or unknowingly, under a thousand names and through a thousand paths. And he styled himself as the Son of that unseen, everlasting source of all life. "Thou art in my heart," he said in one of his hymns, "and no one knoweth Thee save I, Thy Son." And his words, long forgotten, have come down to us, recorded upon the walls of a nobleman's tomb—these amazing words in what is perhaps the earliest poem which can be ascribed with certainty to any particular author: "I, Thy Son…"

Akhenaten is one of the very few men who ever put forth such a bold claim. The aim of this book is to show that, in doing so, he was no less justified than any other teacher of the truth, however impressive may appear the success of the latter contrasted with his defeat; however widespread may be his fame, contrasted with the total oblivion in which has lain the Egyptian king for the last 3,300 years.

«««—»»»

Who is a "son of God"?

There are men who vehemently deny the honor of that title to any person whosoever, in consistency with the fundamental idea of a transcendent God, above and outside the universe and distinct from all that is within it. Others recognize no "Son" but the founder of their own creed, to whom they attribute a miraculous birth as the proof of a divine origin.

In harmony with an entirely different conception of God, I believe that any man who realizes to the full that true relation of his finite individuality to the immanent, impersonal essence of all things can call himself the Son of God—at once human and divine—for the relation of which he is then aware is one of substantial identity with that supreme essence. I also believe that, properly speaking, the word "God" has no meaning except to those who have realized this. Such men are rare, always and everywhere. But they alone stand to justify the existence of the human species.

The aim of this book is to show that Akhenaten was one of those few men, and the earliest known, perhaps, among those whose life can be dated.

«««—»»»

The failure of his teaching to survive him as an established religion can be regarded as one of the tragedies of history. We can explain it; we can even try to redeem it. But the bitter fact remains, for nothing can undo the past.

Other great souls have had disciples to preach their message, martyrs to bear testimony to their greatness in torture and death, missionaries to carry their name and domination to the limits of the earth; they have had commentators, admirers, detractors—philosophers, poets, artists—to keep their memory alive century after century. But Akhenaten's fate was different. He had no sooner died than the fervor of his followers seems to have been spent out. Within a few years, his name was anathematized, his new city pulled down stone by stone, his remains profaned and his memory systematically destroyed, without, apparently, a single cry of protest on the part of any of those 80,000 or more who had, in their zeal, left Thebes with him, 17 years before. Ever since then, until a part of his foreign correspondence and fragments of his hymns were brought to light, some 50 years ago, there was not a man on earth who knew of his existence.

And to this very day, notwithstanding the genuine admiration of a learned few for his rational religion, there are hardly any people in the world whose daily life he fills with his presence.

Why?

Men who are in the habit of judging in haste will at once infer that his teaching cannot have been as perfect as those that have become the nucleus of living faiths.

But success is not the criterion by which one should decide on the value of a religion. In the diffusion of any doctrine far and wide there are too many factors at work for one to be able to ascribe its conquests to the sole amount of truth it contains. Moreover, it is only when that amount of truth appears to be of immediate and tangible use that it appeals to the herd of men sufficiently to help the propagation of the creed. The finer side of every religion is precisely that which escapes the attention and leaves unmoved the sensitiveness of its average followers. Therefore the *number* of people who profess a certain faith, and the extent of the geographical area in which it is recognized, prove nothing.

The *quality* of the nations that officially adhere to it does not stand any better as a guarantee of its value. For it is man who makes religion; not religion that makes man. Through some historic accident—migration, conquest, or the whims of some powerful chief—a sublime teaching can become and remain the collective creed of a pack of gross barbarians. They will no doubt misunderstand it; but they will, none the less, hold sacred the whole mythology and symbolism that tradition has attached to it. And reversely one has seen—and one sees still—cultured, progressive, rationally-trained nations adhere to childish dogmas invented or accepted by their uncritical ancestors. True, they do not fail to produce subtle theologians to interpret the nonsense in terms of hidden wisdom. But nonsense it remains.

A religion should be judged in itself, independently of its real or apparent influence upon any society, apart from its success or failure among men. And its founder—when it has a founder—is the only man whose life and personality one should consider when speaking of it. Judged in that manner, from the sole standpoint of its inner beauty, Akhenaten's simple and rational religion, of which hardly anybody knows, can be compared advantageously with recognized faiths professed by millions of men. And its promoter, with perhaps not more than one or two living disciples, can nevertheless be ranked among the divine souls that honored this earth—among those whom we call "incarnations" or "Sons of God."

《《—》》

We can now try to explain why the worship of Aten failed to endure as an organized collective cult. From the little that can be gathered of it through the existing fragments of Akhenaten's hymns and through the history of his life, one can assert, to say the least, that it was far in advance of the time in which it appeared.

The abyss that separates a man of genius from his contemporaries does not necessarily awe them into accepting his leadership. If it be the result of his superiority in technical knowledge or in skill, it will make him powerful— a hero, a worker of wonders, a giant of war or of industry, whatever be the case. His counsels will soon be followed, and his inventions or discoveries soon admired and put to ever-increasing application because of the obvious advantages that they immediately procure. But if it be the abyss that separates a perfect man from the average human cattle, a rational mind and an enlightened soul from the superstitious crowd of believers; an all-loving, all-understanding heart, from the narrowly selfish majority of men, then, it only helps to render the great one lonely and powerless. The greater the difference between himself and his people, the lesser the immediate success of the man of moral, philosophical or religious genius. His words, his actions meet with no understanding; his lofty example has no imitators; the creation he strives to bring forth remains a dream. To be *technically* in advance of one's time is a source of strength, an assurance of worldly achievements; to be *morally* or *philosophically* ahead of it, is not.

The towering superiority of Akhenaten over his fellow-men has no parallel in the mechanical sphere. "Were it invented to satisfy our modern scientific conceptions, [his religion] could not be logically improved upon at the present day," writes Petrie (1904: 214). Could we imagine a man of the 14th century BC in possession of the secret of our modern airplanes, we would then realize what would have been the mechanical equivalent of Akhenaten's religious revolution. The very idea of it shatters us by its enormity. But, while our imaginary inventor could have safely conquered the world with the help of a single aircraft, the earliest rationalist failed to convince a minimum number of disciples capable of carrying on his work. His teaching "suitable for our own times," met little response in his. Those who could easily have gathered it from his lips and transmitted it to posterity in all its details, were not moved to do so. And we, who would have done so, were not yet born. That is the main reason why nothing was left of it after the 17 glorious years during which it flourished.

There are other reasons for its extinction.

One of them is that the cult of Aten was too rational to appeal to the average people of *any* time. Another is that Akhenaten himself was too good—and perhaps too farsighted, also—to establish it by means of violence.

Three elements seem to have contributed to the propagation of every widespread religion: a mythology; miracles; and a more or less definite doctrine concerning the hereafter. (By "mythology," I mean the true or fictitious story of all natural or supernatural beings connected with the creed: men, angels, beasts, saints, demons, gods, etc.) I do not know of a religion which has stood up to now the test of time without one or two, at least, of these three elements. And most of the great international creeds owe much to all three.

But the cult of Aten seems to have been devoid of all three from the start. That is perhaps why some modern authors have called it a philosophy rather than a religion. But it did possess that stamp of devotion that distinguishes a religion from a philosophy. It was not purely a philosophy, whatever one may say. It even comprised a daily ritual, with hymns and music, incense and flowers. It *was* a religion, but one which offered its followers, at the same time, rational thought, the warmth of devotion, and a stately display of sensuous beauty.

But there were no marvelous tales connected with it. The one theme that could have become the center of a whole literature, had the religion lasted a little longer, was the life of its founder. And that was too simple, too human, too obviously natural to impress the coarse imagination of the commoners.

Akhenaten, in his love of truth, seems to have deliberately stripped himself of all the mystery that had helped his fathers to appear as gods in the eyes of their prostrate people. He was of unconventional manners and of kindly approach. His divinity was not the showy privilege of a Sun-born king, or of a prophet, asserted by external signs, but rather the innermost perfection of a man whose heart, will and understanding were in complete harmony with the eternal laws of life; of a man who had fulfilled man's divine purpose as naturally as others drift away from it. He felt therefore no need of ascertaining it by a fastidious pomp, any more than by strange renunciations. There was no excess in him; nothing that the vulgar eye could look upon as "striking," nothing that popular enthusiasm could catch hold of and magnify. He wrought no extraordinary deeds, as other teachers are said to have done. The only wonder of which he spoke was the everlasting miracle of order and of fertility—the rhythm of day and night, the growth of a bird or of a baby.

And he brought with him, apparently, no new ideas about death, and put no stress upon the ones that were common in Egypt in his time. From the beautiful prayer inlaid upon his coffin, and probably composed by himself, one infers that he believed in the eternal life of the soul. But that is all. No allusion to the nature of that life beyond death, and especially not a single reference to sin, reward and punishment can be found in at least what has survived of the young king's hymns, or in the inscriptions in the tombs of the nobles who boast of having "hearkened to his teaching." Not that the religion of Aten was in any way devoid of a moral character, as some of its modern judges have supposed[1]—a gratuitous assumption, contradicted by the very motto of Akhenaten's life: "Living in Truth." But its morality concerned what one *was* rather than what one did. It was the inherent character of a harmonious life rather than the outcome of any catalogue of "dos" and "don'ts."

As all natural things are, it was foreign to the idea of promises and threats. And that was a reason for it not to appeal to a number of followers. Most men do not want true morality any more than true religion. They want mythologies and miracles to wonder at, and police regulations to abide by; illusions in this world, and punishments and rewards in eternity. In one word, they want eternity made small and exciting to suit the measure of average life. They do not want life simply stripped of its shallowness and made divine—"life in truth." And as Akhenaten had nothing else but that to offer them, his teaching left them indifferent. It did not spread beyond the narrow circle of courtiers.

«««—»»»

The one means by which he could have secured its success as an international creed was violence.

The religion was, indeed, far in advance of its time and of many future ages. And it lacked the elements that generally make a creed popular. Men would, no doubt, have misinterpreted it, misused it, and degraded it within a few years. But it would have spread. Force of money and force of arms can make any people accept any faith, even one that does not suit them. And Akhenaten was both the most powerful and the richest king of his days. I am convinced that, had he chosen to use his strength to impose his new cult upon the world, he would probably have largely succeeded.

But he felt too deeply and he knew too much to sacrifice the spirit of his doctrine to an illusory triumph. Far from using violence to propagate his religion, he did not even persecute those who tried to destroy it. As a result, it is they who enjoyed the thrill of triumph—for the time being. It is they who imposed their will upon the world. They wanted Akhenaten to be cursed, and so he was; they wanted him to be forgotten, and so he was; it was their will that never, never again the world should hear his name, and for over three millennia the world did not.

But his beautiful, rational teaching, however incompletely known, remains unstained by superstition, unmarred by compromise, unconnected

---

[1] Pendlebury (1935: 156-157). See also Budge (1923: 114-115).

with any of the crimes committed, in course of time, in the name of many a successful religion; pure, whole, as its Founder conceived it—a thing of beauty for all ages to come.

«««——»»»

But if there are psychological reasons for which Akhenaten's teaching had little chances of becoming one of the widespread creeds of the world, it could have remained, at least, the religion of an elite. It could have; and it most probably would have, in different surroundings. One of its main features is the diversity of its appeal. It satisfies reason; it fulfils our highest aspirations towards the beautiful; it implies love, not of man alone, but of all creatures. In the midst of general superstition and strife, the better men could have sought in it an ideal to live up to. A pious tradition could have kept the name of Akhenaten sacred to the few who are worthy to know of him.

But such a tradition was never started, or at least never permitted to develop. Egypt, in the 14th century BC, was already too deeply engrossed in formalism to respond to the forgotten message of living life. And the countries around her were either too barbaric or too decadent to understand it. Strangled at home by priestly fanaticism and by popular indifference, the new religion was submerged, abroad, amidst a crowd of conflicting practical faiths that promised men tangible advantages in this world as well as in the next. Persecuted as an organized cult, it soon ceased to exist even as a secret worship. To keep it alive, it would have needed an atmosphere of earnestness and of toleration, a truly religious atmosphere as it was difficult to find anywhere on earth for many centuries, except perhaps among a minority of Hindus.

We may observe here that none of the lofty doctrines of antiquity which originated before Christianity have survived, west of India. And, unexpected as this may seem, India might well be the only land that would have given the youthful worshipper of radiant energy a place worthy of him in his time, had she heard of his teaching; the only land, also, who probably would have continued to venerate him to this very day as one of the incarnations of the Supreme Soul.

«««——»»»

I believe that no teaching would meet, better than his, the exigencies of the critical modern mind. Yet, it is not my intention to try to revive it on a broad scale, as the basis of a public cult. I do not think it desirable to attempt what its founder himself does not seem to have aimed at—he who, though fully conscious of its universal value, did not try to explain it to the many.

With all their pride in progress, our times are no less foolish and no less barbaric than his. We now use electric fans, while in Thebes they did not; that is about all the difference. The resuscitated religion of cosmic energy would soon offer, in the hands of any crowd, as ludicrous a sight as that of the great "living" faiths of today. We do not wish to rob the other world-teachers of a few millions of insignificant admirers in order to give a noisy following to the great man who is dear to us. We know too well, through daily experience, what the quality of that following would be.

But I do wish to make the name and teaching of Akhenaten popular among the best of our contemporaries—among those who really represent the higher tendencies of our skeptical and at the same time mystical age; among those to whom dogmas no longer appeal, whom wonders no longer impress, whom religion without a background of positive knowledge, and science without the feeling of the seriousness of life, leave equally unsatisfied. It is among such people that I earnestly wish to revive the spirit of him who, a thousand years before Socrates and nearly 900 years before the Buddha, united the boldest rationalistic views to the deep intuitive certitude of the oneness of God, the oneness of Life, and the brotherhood of all creatures.

Modern scholars have already recognized his undeniable greatness. The earliest and most eminent of all those specialists who have labored to revive his memory among the learned, Flinders Petrie, has paid him a magnificent tribute.[2] But what I want also is that Akhenaten's name be held sacred by all those who, without being scholars, can think in terms of truth and feel in terms of beauty, and who are capable of modeling their lives on an immortal example of living perfection.

More so, if few be likely to live up to the spirit of his teaching, let all at least know that there has been such a man as he, once, long long ago. Let them remain superstitious, vulgar and violent, if they will; but let them know that there has been a man in whose life religion and reason walked hand in hand; a man whose very being was harmony, balance, supreme elegance, and who lost an empire for the sake of truth. Few meditate upon the beauty of the Sun; yet all behold it. Above man's unchanging mediocrity He shines in glory. In a similar manner, worshipped by a few, but familiar to all after 3,300 years of silence, I want the name of Akhenaten, Son of the Sun, young forever, to live once more in the consciousness of our old world.

This will no doubt appear as a stupendous dream.

The aim of this book is to make others feel that the dream will become true the moment they sincerely realize its beauty.

---

[2] In his *History of Egypt* (1904: 214, 218). Also see his *Tell-el-Amarna* (1894: 41-42).

PART I:

THE WORLD'S FIRST INDIVIDUAL

Fig. 2: Akhenaten and Nefertiti.

CHAPTER 1

FLEUR SÉCULAIRE [1]

Akhenaten was born in Thebes, in about 1365 BC, in a world already as old, as civilized, and as sophisticated as our own. And he was the son of the greatest monarch of that world; the last offspring, in direct descent, of a long and glorious line of warriors over-loaded with the spoils of conquest; the heir of an empire that stretched, in modern words, from the Sudan to the borders of Armenia, and of a culture more than four thousand years old.

When he was a child, the famous Pyramids of Giza were already well over one thousand years old. So too the first empire-builder of whom we know something definite—Sargon of Akkad. And beyond the glories of which the oldest monuments bore witness, and beyond the mighty shadows of half-forgotten heroes and king-gods lost in the midst of legend, a still remoter antiquity, with its immemorial art and wisdom, extended over centuries, down to the dim beginnings of the Neolithic Age, and further still. Crete and the Aegean Isles had flourished for over two thousand years, and Babylonia and Elam for several millennia more, while, unaware of each other and of the rest of mankind, distant India and China counted long centuries of polished life.

If, indeed, instead of letting ourselves be over-impressed by the few hundreds of years that separate us from him, we stop to consider the endless length of time that separates both Akhenaten and ourselves from the mysterious origins of civilization, we might well look upon him as a man of yesterday, almost as one of our contemporaries.

He was the tenth Pharaoh of that glorious Eighteenth Dynasty which opens the period known in history as the "New Kingdom."

His ancestors, the kings of Thebes, had freed Egypt from foreign domination; his great-great-grandfather had made her the head of an empire; his father had made her the abode of unprecedented splendor.

Sporadic revolts in Nubia (Ethiopia) and in Syria had been utterly crushed, and peace had at last succeeded the unceasing struggles of the former reigns. From all parts of the immense empire, tribute in gold and silver, in ivory and slaves and cedar wood, poured in regularly. King Amenhotep III,

---

[1] "Secular flower."

whom some modern writers have rightly called Amenhotep the Magnificent, lived a life of pleasure in the midst of every kind of luxury, with a number of beautiful wives and concubines collected from every country of the known world.

The granaries were full and the people content. Thousands of foreign slaves—the prize of war—were toiling for the welfare of Egypt: tilling the fields, digging or repairing canals, extracting gold from the Nubian mines, dragging down the Nile huge barges loaded with granite, building temples and palaces, and keeping the highways in good condition. And the faraway kings of Babylon and of Mitanni—the Pharaoh's brothers-in-law—and the king of the Hittites and the king of barbaric Assyria wrote with equal greedy envy, in their dispatches to Amenhotep III: "Verily, in thy land, gold is as common as dust."

Every refinement in pleasure, every treasure of art, every subtlety of thought, every comfort, every delicacy, every brilliancy was to be found in Thebes. Nothing equaled the beauty of its monuments, the pomp of its festivities, the wealth of its priests who enjoyed throughout the world a reputation of mysterious powers and of hidden wisdom. Its temples, of which the gigantic ruins still stir the admiration of travelers, stood then in all their glory. Their half-dark halls inspired something of that sacred awe that one feels in the cave-temples of medieval India; and their rows of mighty pillars with lotus-shaped capitals displayed already that harmony of proportions, that grace blended with majesty, that perfect elegance that was one day to distinguish the art of Periclean Greece.

Thebes was not merely the metropolis of the greatest empire then existing, not merely one of the largest and most sumptuous cities that the world had ever seen; it was the masterpiece in which the genius of the Near and Middle East had finally expressed itself, after having groped for centuries in quest of perfection. It seemed as though nothing could be added to its beauty.

It seemed, also, as though nothing could be added to its glory.

Along with the words of praise to all the gods that covered the walls and columns, the crowds of worshippers that thronged the halls of the temple of Karnak could read in golden hieroglyphics, on a slab of black granite, the song of war and triumph of King Thotmose III, the words of the Theban god to the maker of Egypt's greatness:

I have come; I have granted thee to trample over the great ones of Syria;
I have hurled them beneath thy sandals in their lands...

It is one of the most beautiful hymns of victory of all times. Its echo had run through the world from the Nile Valley to the Black Sea and to the Persian Gulf, from the Libyan Desert to the boundaries of India. And as he beheld the solemn words, the Egyptian pilgrim was filled with national pride. What song would ever efface the glory of that one?

Thus, in wealth, in splendor, and in warrior-like fame stood Thebes, the capital of the first nation of the earth, the seat of divine royalty, the proud City of Amun, the mighty god. Millennia of culture had created it; the skill of all known lands had adorned it. And the sword of its kings had spread far and wide the glory of its name and the terror of its local deity whom the priests had boldly identified with Re, the immemorial Sun-god of the Egyptians.

It is then that he came.

Birth of the King

On the western bank of the Nile, upon a site which to this day retains its loveliness, was built the Charuk palace, the residence of the Pharaoh Amenhotep III.

It was a light but beautiful structure of brick and precious wood, decorated with exquisite paintings and surrounded by immense gardens full of shade and full of peace.

From the terraces of the palace one beheld to the east, beyond the Nile and its palm-groves, white walls contrasted with dark shadows, flat roofs of different levels, flights of steps, broad avenues and gardens and monumental gates: all that glory that was Thebes. In the foreground, the towering pylons of the great temple of Amun emerged above the outer walls of the sacred enclosure that stretched over miles. And the gilded tops of innumerable obelisks glittered in the dazzling light or glowed like red-hot embers in the purple of sunset. One could distinguish many other temples dedicated to all the gods of Upper and Lower Egypt, temples with doors of bronze and gates of granite, of which the humblest would have been the pride of any other city. To the west, the eye wandered over the vastness of the desert.

It is in that palace that Akhenaten was born.

His mother, Queen Tiye, was the chief wife of Amenhotep III, and one of the ablest women of all times. While her weary lord, after experiencing in his long life of pleasure the vanity of all pursuits, had gradually brushed aside the tiresome duties of kingship, it was she who received the foreign ambassadors, gave orders to provincial governors, and drafted the dispatches that messengers were to carry to Babylon or to the faraway capital of the Hittites. It was she who, through a well-organized network of informers, kept an eye on the restless vassal princelings of Syria as well as on the movements of the unconquered tribes below the Fourth Cataract of the Nile. It was she who saw to it that the public officers did their work well, and that the taxes came in without delay.

Consort of the mightiest monarch, and the virtual ruler of his empire no less than the head of his "house of women," she had enjoyed all through her

26 years of married life every pleasure, every luxury, and every glory that a woman can imagine in her wildest dreams. For her the gardens around the Charuk palace had been extended and adorned at great cost with an artificial lake. For her the priests of the oldest Sun-god, Re—which they also called Aten, the Disk, in the sacred city of Heliopolis (or 'On'), his abode—enjoyed favor at court, in spite of the secret jealousy of the powerful priests of Amun, for the god of Heliopolis was Tiye's favorite god. In pomp and power the queen's years had drifted away. She was fairly past 35, and perhaps not far from 40, when at last she bore the little prince.

The babe's coming into the world was greeted by the joy of a whole nation. Sacrifices of thanksgiving were offered to the gods of Egypt; distant vassals from North and South welcomed through their messengers the child who was one day to be their lord, and allied monarchs congratulated the king, his father, in friendly dispatches.

But the birth of Akhenaten was a greater event than anyone in his days could realize. The world was already old, as I have said—as old as it is now. Men had already invented many arts and many gods, and built up many kingdoms. The infant who, in the Charuk palace, now smiled for the first time to the Sun, was, in a few years, to transcend the very idea of nation, to preach the oneness and universality of the principle of all existence, and to show men the way of life in truth, which is also life in beauty—life divine upon earth. That he was to proclaim—less by his words than by his deeds, less by his deeds than by his attitude towards things—which the weary world had dimly sought, age after age; which those who know him not are still seeking: the synthesis of total knowledge and perfect love.

His life, which had just begun, was to last very little indeed: less than three decades. Yet, in that short span of time, he was to be what neither the victories of his fathers, nor the wealth and wisdom of his country, nor the arts and glories of all the ancient kingdoms had succeeded in producing: a perfect Individual of equal genius and sanctity—a divine Man.

His mother, who had grown-up daughters, may well have looked upon his birth as the fulfillment of her long, active and sumptuous life. It was, in no less manner, the culmination of a long evolution towards the rational and the beautiful, the ultimate achievement of the oldest cultures of the world, already so fruitful in outstanding creations. Like unto the cactus-tree which, so they say, blooms after a hundred years into one resplendent flower that lasts less than a day, Egypt had lived and dreamt and toiled four thousand years, and mankind perhaps 50 times longer, in order to produce him whose life was to remain in history only a flash—but a flash of unsurpassed beauty.

Fig. 3: Sculpture of Akhenaten, excavated at Karnak (Cairo Museum).

CHAPTER 2

Prince Amenhotep

There is no historical record of Akhenaten's life before he succeeded his father as king of Egypt. What we know definitely about him at an earlier date is very little. We know, for instance, that his parents had conceived him in an advanced age, and that he was given at his birth the name of Amenhotep—his father's name—which means "Amun is at rest," or "Amun is pleased." The name under which he is famous in history he chose himself later on. We know that he was, as a baby, committed to the care of a woman—the "great royal nurse"—who bore, like the queen herself, the name of Tiye, and was the wife of Ay, a court dignitary and a priest. We know also that he was married, some time before his father's death, to a princess called Nefertiti, of whom it is not certain whether she was an Egyptian or a foreigner. That is practically all that can be gathered from the written documents so far brought to light, about the first part of a life so remarkable.

But if nothing precise can be stated about the facts of those early years, yet, from what we know of Amenhotep III's "house of women" and its inmates, something can be inferred of the atmosphere in which the royal child was brought up. And something, too, we can expect to guess of his first reactions to the world around him, in light of all that we know of his subsequent life.

To say that he was the son of parents of mature age is already to suggest some prominent traits of his personality, such as eagerness, seriousness of mind, depth. To add that he was not, like most babies, the casual product of a moment's fancy, but the fruit of yearning and of prayer no less than of pleasure, not only accepted but intensely desired. To recall that his mother—herself an exceptional woman—with all her power and glory, with the love of her lord and the graceful presence of several daughters was not happy until he, a son, was born to her. That she longed for him, year after year, as for the one blessing she could dream of, is to explain how he was no average child, and could never grow into an average man.

The queen, as I have said, was surely over 35, and perhaps not far from 40 at the time of his birth—an age which is not young for a woman in any climate, and which, in the tropics, in the days of Egypt's greatness just as now, was considered old. We may try to imagine her feelings when she came to know that she was once more to become a mother, long after her daughters had grown up. Imagine her joy for an event that had so long seemed unlikely, if not impossible, and then the hopes, the dreams she had concerning him who was not yet born. Imagine the prayers she addressed to the most powerful gods and goddesses, especially to her favorite deities, for the welfare and future greatness of her child. Those ardent hopes, those dreams, that fervor of prayer, that constant anxious thought concentrated on him in an expectation of glorious days to come, were the very earliest influences upon the formation of Akhenaten's personality.

TIYE: QUEEN MOTHER

The god whom Tiye worshipped was Aten—the Disk—the oldest Sun-god of Egypt. The seat of his venerable cult was not Thebes, but the sacred city of Heliopolis—"the city of the obelisk"—which the Greeks were one day to call "the city of the Sun." The priests of Heliopolis were less wealthy but more thoroughly versed in ancient wisdom than those of Thebes. For a generation or two they had been trying to make their deity popular in the great metropolis, and especially at court. They hoped that, if they succeeded, the god would recover all over Egypt the prominent place which he held of old. And they had succeeded to some extent. People were beginning to add to the name of the mighty Amun, in votive inscriptions, that of the elder god.

And when he had inaugurated the newly-built artificial lake in the gardens around his palace, the Pharaoh had named the pleasure-boat in which he had glided over its waters 'Tehen-Aten,' i.e. "Aten gleams."

But the name of Aten was still that of a secondary god among many. Tiye herself was far from looking upon him as the only god worth praying to; she had grown up, like everybody else, in a world full of various deities, and her father, Yuaa, was a priest of Min, the fertility-god. Yet she was impressed by the great antiquity of the cult of the Disk. Perhaps also did she realize, with her sharp intelligence, that there was much more in the less popular religious traditions of the priests of Heliopolis than in the pious devices that the ministers of Amun in Thebes were in the habit of using to impress the people, and sometimes to force their will upon the kings. She probably disliked their increasing grip upon public affairs and, without wishing to displease them openly, she dreamt within her heart of a new order of things more in accordance with the rights of royalty. Perhaps she had already the dim presentment of a possible conflict between Aten and Amun, as of a struggle of royalty against priest-craft.

Whatever might have been her aspirations at the moment, there can be little doubt that they colored her conception of her child's greatness. And he would be a providential child, a man the like of which are born once in many hundreds of years. He would put an end to the arrogance of the priests of Amun, restore on a wide scale the cult of the old Sun-god of Heliopolis, reassert the meaning of divine kingship, and surpass in power and glory all his forefathers.

Were these the thoughts of Queen Tiye while, day after day, she felt the unborn prince come into being within her body? It is impossible to say. All one can state is that it was natural for a woman with her ambitions to entertain such thoughts and that, if she did so, her hopes were to be rewarded a hundredfold—though not in the way she might have expected.

YOUTH AND CHILDHOOD

The young prince spent his early years in his father's "house of women." To judge by what we know of his health all through his life, and also by some of the portraits of his boyhood, he was probably a delicate if not a sickly baby, perhaps also a premature one. Though, as I repeat, there is no information to be gathered concerning the very first part of his life, we may imagine him, when four or five years old, as a quiet, slender boy with a long neck, delicate features, large dreamy eyes, pretty hands like those of a girl, and nothing of the boisterousness of ordinary children of his age.

The uncompromising spirit that he showed, hardly ten years later, as a king, leads us to believe that he already had a strong personality, and that he was conscious of it. And that he loved truth and was incapable of dissimulation. This must have urged him, more than once, to rebel against whatever shocked him or simply bored him; to speak when he was not expected to, and often to take a hasty initiative in matters which the grown-ups preferred to reserve for themselves. It is likely, too, that he never obeyed but those whom he really loved, and then only after asking many "whys" and "what-fors." In a word, if conventional behavior be the measure of what is "good," then many a well-intentioned pedagogue might have called him a "naughty child." That much-used adjective is equally applied to children who are worse and to others who are better than their environment. Prince Amenhotep was of the latter.

EARLY INFLUENCES

The greatest and most lasting influence to exert itself upon the royal child was surely that of his mother. His father, who had prematurely grown old, loved him, no doubt, who was his only son and heir. But he had put in him less hopes, less dreams than the queen had, for he was himself weary, and took less interest than she did in the future, even in the present. It was several years since he had practically let the burden of government lie upon his able chief-wife, whom he knew he could trust. It is probable that he also relied entirely on her for the education of his son.

As already stated, the queen was a worshipper of the solar god of Heliopolis, Aten—the Disk. She must have taught the child to render homage to him at sunrise and sunset. The boy, who was born an artist, opened his heart to the beauty of the Sun.

It is likely that many times his mother's sweet words rang in tune with his rapture in front of a glowing sky, in which the Disk appeared or disappeared. He saw the fiery reflection of the Sun upon her face, which it beautified, while she repeated to him, in a tender voice, something of what the wise men of Heliopolis and her own common sense had taught her about the beneficent Lord of the Two Horizons. He watched the birds fly round and round, with joyous thrills, as the Sun flooded the gardens, the Nile, and the western hills with pink morning light, and the queen told him that they were glad because He, the Father of all creatures, had come back. She showed him in the ponds the water-flowers that had just opened to receive His warm kiss. And he looked at them, and understood that they were alive, like himself. And he loved them, and loved the birds and the beasts and the many-colored insects, and all things that live and feel the Sun's caress.

It is true that the history of his early years is not recorded. Even if it were, would history have remembered to note the small facts of daily life, psychologically so important? Yet, one can well imagine Prince Amenhotep, a delicate and sensitive child, stooping to pick up a fledgling fallen from its nest, because he felt for the fragile drop of life, or smoothing down with his little hands the burning-hot fur of a cat lying in the sun and enjoying to see how, while it purred, it kept gazing at the faraway Disk with its half-shut emerald eyes. He loved the Sun as a living and loving God, and, being by nature kind to living creatures, he loved them all the more, in Him. His mother encouraged him in that true, spontaneous piety, so different from the vain display of bigotry she had so often witnessed among grown-up people. And the Disk, of which he was one day to evolve a personal conception more lofty than anything Tiye could dream of, was always to retain, in his subconscious mind, the indefinable charm of things we have loved from childhood.

The queen, however, was no monotheist, and surely no philosopher. It would be a great mistake to attribute to her early influence the essential of Akhenaten's religious ideas. They were decidedly his own. The only thing that one can say is that his mother was one of the factors which helped him, from the very beginning, to find his way. That she did, and no more. But that was enough.

And besides the positive influence she exerted by directing him to ponder over the beauty of the Sun, she played also a negative part, equally important. She helped to create around him the psychological conditions in which the whole religion of Egypt, with the exception of the ancient Heliopolitan solar cult, would appear to him the least lovable. She did not create the facts that would have impressed him anyhow as he grew to know them: the dead ceremonial of the temples of Amun, "as intellectually low and primitive," in the words of Weigall (1923: 81), "as its state of organization was high and pompous." There was the hypocrisy of the priests, whose piety was dwindling as their wealth and power increased. And there was the superstition of the people, and that narrow national pride which, kindled by constant victories, had become more and more aggressive since the liberation of the country from the yoke of the Hyksos.

But, willingly or unwillingly, she probably drew his attention to some of those facts as soon as he could think. And even earlier still, stray remarks of hers about the priests of Amun, whom she did not like, and about their impressive tricks, which she probably detested, must have made it impossible for him to feel, towards those sacred persons, the respect that generations of princes had felt; impossible even for him, perhaps, to take their faith seriously.

It is quite plausible to suppose that on more than one occasion the child, who was extremely intelligent, overheard such bitter remarks. Moreover, he was soon given preceptors who, apart from reading and writing and the elements of the sciences of his age, taught him what he should know of the history of his fathers. In a country in which everything was calculated to impress upon the future king the consciousness of his divine origin, every mark of supernatural favor shown by the gods to his family must have been stressed to the utmost. And Prince Amenhotep was surely told of such miracles as that, for instance, which occurred under Queen Hatshepsut, when during a solemn procession the statue of Amun suddenly stopped in front of him who was to succeed the queen as Thotmose III, and nodded to him before everybody, so as to make the choice of heaven manifest. The story seemed suitable enough to inspire the child with reverence for the Theban god as well as for his illustrious great-great-grandfather, the builder of the Egyptian empire.

What impression it made upon him, nobody knows. But we do know that the prince was to show a very critical mind in early adolescence. And that is enough for one to hold it possible that, already as a child, he only half-believed the marvelous tale. His next step was probably to ask his mother about it, in answer of which she told him that the whole scene had been staged by the priests of Amun, who favored Thotmose III as Queen Hatshepsut's successor. She added, perhaps, that when he grew up, he would acquire still more glory than his great ancestor if only he succeeded in keeping those same priests in their place, for they were now becoming a nuisance to royal power. And she spoke emphatically, for she felt what she said.

Prayers, ceremonies, sacrifices in honor of the "king of gods" were, of course, a part and parcel of the young prince's official life, so to say. As heir-apparent, he had to be present wherever his presence was considered necessary. He was never taught that Aten was the only god. And for some years at least it appears that he did not question the existence of other deities. Yet, his early devotion to the Disk must have had the natural exclusiveness of every ardent love. Those dutiful attendances to shrines of other gods must have seemed boring to him, to say the least, in spite of the surrounding pomp. And his inborn disposition to tell the truth and to act according to his feelings must have made him feel morally uncomfortable every time he was forced to be the silent witness of some priestly magic on grand occasions, or to pay a public homage to Amun, the god whom he seems never to have loved.

It has been said that every great life is the realization of a child's dream. In the case of Akhenaten, who was little more than a child when he began to put his ideas into action, this is obvious. But it is likely that he conceived his main ideas before he gave them a public expression, and that the great tendencies which were to direct his astonishing career were discernible in him long before he even had ideas. That is to say that his contempt for Amun and for most of the national gods, and his passionate adoration of the Sun alone, are probably to be traced to an incredibly early age. His whole life being a marvel of precocity, there is nothing unnatural in supposing him to have been a "heretic" from the start.

A WORLDVIEW EVOLVES

One may assume that, besides his mother, the prince's step-mothers had a place in his early life. We know next to nothing about them, but we know at least that they were numerous and that they came from various countries far and near. One of the wives of Amenhotep III was the sister of the ruling king of Babylon; another, named Gilukhipa, was the sister of Dushratta, the ruling king of Mitanni. Apart from her, the Pharaoh had married at least one other Mitannian princess and a number of women from all the countries of the Near East, especially from Syria and Mesopotamia. Alliances with foreign ladies of rank were no longer uncommon in the royal family of Egypt since Thotmose IV had taken Mutemuya, the daughter of Artatama, king of Mitanni, as his chief wife.

The part played in the prince's religious education by the Mitannian inmates of his father's harem, however, must have been minimal.[1] Of course, it is plausible to imagine the royal child coming to know from the mouth of his step-mothers the names and legends of different gods. And it is possible

---

[1] The proper explanation of the doubtless striking similitude between his conception of Divinity and that of the Aryans of India, as expressed in the Rig-Veda, lies, not in the assumption of any influence exerted upon Akhenaten, but in the fact that he was himself partly Aryan (being the grandson of a Mitannian princess).

that some of those glimpses of foreign religion, especially under its solar aspects, made a greater impression on him than others. It is also not impossible that he might have heard on some occasions of a sun-god little different, at least in his superficial features, from the Surya of the Aryans and from the god he was himself to praise one day under the name of Aten. But the point remains doubtful, for lack of information. And the impression the prince received must have been rather vague, anyhow. For even if there did exist any noteworthy solar philosophy behind the sun-gods of the Mitannians, it is doubtful whether any of the Pharaoh's wives or concubines would have been able to convey adequately the essence of it, especially to a child.

It is much more natural to imagine that the young prince, popular among his step-mothers because of his mild disposition and girlish beauty, gladly used to go to their rooms. Surely he spent his time there playing, chatting about trifling things, as children do—partaking of the sweets they gave him. And no doubt he occasionally listened to some outlandish tale of gods and demons, of heroes and hidden treasures and fairy-like queens, tales such as have always been told to little boys and girls all over the world.

Knowing of the child's precocious understanding, I am inclined to believe that he loved stories and also that he readily put questions to his step-mothers, and to any foreigners he would meet, about strange lands and customs. We do not know if anybody ever threw into his subconscious mind the idea of a foreign sun-god with some of the attributes he was one day to transfer to Aten, or if the god of the priests of Heliopolis, of which he knew well, was sufficient to set him dreaming lofty religious dreams.

But we may say that, through his daily contact with his step-mothers, Prince Amenhotep acquired one thing at least which was to leave upon him an indelible impression: the knowledge that every land had a sun-god. That is, no doubt, the one important thing he learnt, at a very tender age, from Gilukhipa and the other ladies of the royal harem—Mitannians, Babylonians, Syrians and Canaanites, Libyans and Nubians, women from the Upper Euphrates and from the Arabian desert and from the sacred land of Punt; Cretans also, possibly, and women from the Aegean Isles, perhaps even from farther northern shores, who had all brought their gods with them.

There were not only sun-gods, it is true. Every land had also its moon-god, and its war-god, and many other gods and goddesses in great numbers, some of which could more or less be paralleled with those of Egypt. Another intelligent child would have remarked that all the gods were universal, and universally made in the image of their worshippers. And he would have stopped there and troubled himself no longer about the nature of Godhead. The child who was one day to be Akhenaten probably made the same remarks. But he did not stop there. For along with that keen, analytical, destructive intelligence with which he was soon to crush all man-made gods, there was in him an immense power of devotion which he had already directed to the one God whose beauty overwhelmed him—the Sun. Among the hosts of deities of which he gradually came to know, the Sun alone he chose to see. And he saw Him everywhere, for everywhere He was present. He was the true God of all nations.

And as from the terraces of his palace the child gazed day after day at the real Sun and watched Him rise and set in incandescent splendor, strange thoughts came to him—thoughts that no boy of his age, and perhaps no grown-up man had ever had before. That Sun—the Disk, the god of his mother—was surely not a god like the others, not even like those who were supposed to represent Him. How could indeed those clumsy sun-gods be really the same as He? Since all nations saw the Sun in heaven, why then did they not look up to Him directly, instead of making themselves graven images so unworthy of Him?

No one knows what age he was when he first put such questions to himself. It may have been a few years before his accession to the throne—that is to say, when he was a mere child. Children do, sometimes, open new horizons of thought for themselves. But their best intuitions are, half the time, crushed by so-called "education." Prince Amenhotep's intuition of the oneness of God, which he grasped through the visible Sun, was too strong to be crushed. As he grew in years, he more often and more thoughtfully gazed at the sky—the very image of glowing oneness—and became more and more devoted to the life-giving Disk, the one God whom he loved. And a time must have come when what had been at first, in him, a dim desire, burst forth into a determination that nothing could bend. At that time, he resolved to use it for the glorification of his God.

EDUCATION AND REBELLION

The prince's education was confided to learned men, mostly if not entirely chosen among the priests. We know nothing of the curriculum followed in his studies, but it is plausible to imagine that the sciences the most in honor in Egypt—mathematics and astronomy on one hand, and the history of the past on the other—had a prominent place in his program. Apart from his mother-tongue, he was probably taught Babylonian, which was the international medium of trade and diplomacy for centuries and the language in which kings wrote to one another. It is likely that he was able to speak, possibly also to read, several other languages. Brought up as he was in the crowded harem of his father, where so many nations and tribes were represented, it seems hardly believable that he was not. Much less gifted children get acquainted with foreign speeches with amazing facility.

The method of teaching in Egypt, 1400 years before Christ, was not much different from that which prevails to this very day in the Mohammedan schools of the same country, and in the East in general; nay, from that used in Europe throughout the Middle Ages. It consisted mainly of making the child repeat over and over again, until he knew it by heart, all what it was not absolutely necessary to explain to him thoroughly, that is to say, all his curriculum save mathematics. And young Prince Amenhotep was probably made to learn in that manner whole scrolls of hieroglyphics.

There can be also no doubt that the prince's preceptors thoroughly insisted upon the protection which Amun, the patron god of Thebes and of the Dynasty, had bestowed so lavishly upon all his forefathers. For however popular the ancient god Aten had re-become at court on account of the queen's devotion, Amun remained the great god of the land, and Prince Amenhotep was expected to be, like all his ancestors, his loyal servant—in fact, his first priest.

In the light of what we already know of the royal child's tendencies, we may now try to picture ourselves how he probably reacted to the education thus given him.

First, the very method of teaching is likely to have made much of the imparted knowledge appear to him as uninteresting. The wise but commonplace maxims and proverbs and the sacred hymns he was probably made to repeat in paying great attention to subtle rules of cadence and pronunciation, must have stirred less joy in his heart and conveyed to him less meaning than did the song of a bird, the music of a shepherd's flute in the distance, or a single glimpse of blue sky. Like most children who are all-round intelligent, Prince Amenhotep had little taste for bookish knowledge devoid of the touch of life. He may have grasped it easily; and we have indeed no reasons to suppose he did not. But one may doubt if it interested him. The main distinctive traits of his mind, relentless logic and poetic enthusiasm, so remarkable in the man, were certainly prominent already in the child. He must have liked all that could set in motion his reasoning power or captivate his imagination. And, as far as we can infer, the manner in which he was taught could do neither.

On the other hand, it is likely that he used to put to his preceptors many embarrassing questions and that he made, now and then, remarks which already revealed his triple genius as a forerunner of modern science, as an artist, and as a saint.

There are no means of knowing what those remarks were. Possibly, as I have suggested, the prince compared more than once the ungainly figure of several of the deities he knew with the radiant beauty of the real Sun-disk, which he adored. Possibly, when told that the crocodile-headed god, Sebek, was another manifestation of Re, the Sun, he refused to believe it on aesthetic grounds. Possibly, too, when urged to pay more attention to the moon-god,

Khonsu—the son of the great Amun—he may have retorted that the moon only shines by the reflected light of the Sun, without knowing how rigorously true his statement was. It would be too much to attribute such an intuition as this to any other child without sound historic evidence. It is not distorting the spirit of history to hold it possible, even likely, in a child who was, but a few years later, to grasp intuitively the fundamental equivalence of light and heat.

Finally, if there be anything true in the belief that the basic aversions of an individual appear very early in life, we may suppose that Prince Amenhotep always showed a particular repulsion for acts of cruelty of any sort. It seems, for instance, impossible for his gentle nature not to have shrunk as he heard of the well-known torture of the seven Syrian chiefs captured by Amenhotep II during his campaign and hung, head downwards, in front of that Pharaoh's galley, as it sailed triumphantly up the Nile. The idea of those same men solemnly sacrificed to Amun, and of their bloody remains left to rot for days upon the walls of Thebes and of Napata, must have filled him with hardly less disgust. And whatever be the spirit in which they were related to him, such accounts have perhaps contributed no little to infuse into him, for life, the horror of war; to thwart in him every desire of imperial expansion at such a cost; and to turn his indifference towards the national god Amun into positive hatred.

NEFERTITI, PRINCESS OF LIGHT

Some time before his accession, Prince Amenhotep, then hardly more than ten years old, was married with all the customary pomp to a little princess, Nefertiti.

Scholars do not agree about the bride's parentage. Petrie (1904: 207) identifies her with Tadukhipa, daughter of Dushratta, king of Mitanni. Weigall (1922: 49) rejects this view on account of the princess's "typically Egyptian" features, and supposes her to be the daughter of Ay, a court dignitary. The striking resemblance between her portraits and those of her young husband has prompted others to suggest that she was his half, or even his full sister.[2] Brother and sister marriages were common in Egypt, as everyone knows.

I have no opinion to express on the subject. Yet, I find it difficult to dismiss Petrie's version on the sole ground of Nefertiti's looks. For, if the princess were indeed the daughter of Dushratta, then her mother would be the sister and her paternal grandmother, the paternal aunt of Amenhotep III, while the prince's paternal grandmother—the chief wife of Thotmose IV—was, as we know, Dushratta's paternal aunt. In other words, the wedded children would be even more closely related than ordinary first cousins are, and there would be nothing strange in their resembling each other as brother and sister.

---

[2] For example, Budge (1923: 76); Baikie (1926: 243); Hall (1936: 258).

However, it makes little difference whose daughter Nefertiti actually was. To history, she remains Akhenaten's beloved consort. It is curious to observe that her beauty, revealed in her famous limestone portrait-busts—the loveliest masterpieces of Egyptian sculpture—has made her far more widely known than her great husband to the modern European public at large.

It is probable that the idyllic love that was to bind the prince and his consort together all through their years began long before their actual connubial life. If the features and more particularly the expression of the face do reveal something of what we call the soul, then we must suppose that the two children, heir-apparent and future queen of Egypt, had much in common. Their earliest portraits represent them both with the same regular, oval face, slender neck and large, dark eyes full of yearning; with already, in their gaze, a touch of thoughtful sadness which is not of their age. A delicate, almost feminine charm seems to have distinguished Akhenaten's person all his life. But it was balanced in latter days, as his portraits testify, by a stamp of manly determination. In early youth, and especially in childhood, before his struggle with the surrounding world had actually begun, his virile qualities had not yet found their expression; the delicate charm alone was prominent; and the newly-married prince resembled his wife even more than he did in subsequent years.

The two played together, sat and read or looked at pictures together, listened together to the stories that grown-up people told them. They admired together a lotus-bud that had just opened; they watched a velvety butterfly on a rose, or a flight of swallows going north with the coming of hot weather. A painted bas-relief, dating perhaps a few years later, pictures the prince leaning gracefully on a staff while Nefertiti gives him a bunch of flowers to smell. An indefinable sweetness pervades the whole scene, which we may plausibly take to be a faithful likeness of the young couple's everyday life.

It is probable, too, that Prince Amenhotep soon initiated his child-wife into what could already be called his higher life. Whatever be her parentage, the worship of the Sun was nothing new to the little princess. But through her daily contact with the inspired child with whom she was now wedded, what had meant to her, until then, little more than a mere succession of grown-up people's gestures, became an act of personal love. Although his own ideas were yet far from definite, Prince Amenhotep probably taught her to see the Sun as he did, that is to say, as the most beautiful and the kindest of gods; we do not know if we should add, at this early stage of his religious history: as the only God worth praising.

If Nefertiti be, as Petrie suggests, the daughter of the king of Mitanni, then one may suppose that she told her young husband about Mithra and perhaps Surya, the sun-gods of her country, and that she described to him in a clumsy manner, putting too much stress upon details, as children do, some of the rites with which they were worshipped there. It is doubtful whether there could be in those details, as she presented them, anything impressive enough to be of psychological importance in the prince's evolution. But he may have seized the opportunity to tell the little girl, pointing to the fiery Disk in heaven, that this was the only real Sun, under whatever name and in whatever way one may praise Him in different lands. And she possibly felt that there was truth in his childish remarks, and began to look up to him as to somebody very wise—wiser even, perhaps, than the grown-up people.

A MOST EXCEPTIONAL YOUNG MAN

I have tried to emphasize that, before becoming the founder of the Religion of the Disk, Akhenaten was once a child with many of the weaknesses natural to his age, but, at the same time, a child in whom the first sparks of genius must often have burst forth; a child whose coming greatness must have appeared, at times, undoubtable.

As there is hardly any information about his early years to be gathered from historical records, one has to be content with imagining what expression the main emotional tendencies must have taken in the prince, as a little boy, the qualities of mind, and traits of character which made his life and teaching, as a king, what we know them to be. But one can assert with a high degree of probability that those psychological elements were already observable in him at an extremely early age, and that he was therefore not a child like others.

It is likely that he was a serious, meditative child, full of the vague call of an Unknown that he could not yet think about, but that he could feel at times with strange intensity. He had vivid, delicate sensations, and was already deeply moved by visible beauty—even more so, as far as we can infer, by that of land, water and sky, and of living creatures, than by that of the highly artistic luxuries in the midst of which he was growing up. He was a sensitive and loving child, who would burst out in indignant rage at the report, not to speak of the sight, of any act of brutality committed, with whatever purpose it be, on man or beast. He was an exceedingly logical child, who would question the very foundation of whatever did not seem evident to him. He who would never be content with such evasive answers as grown-up-people often give to children who discuss, in order to make them keep silent.

Above all, if there be any children who, from the day they were born, have never told a lie or acted deceitfully, he was certainly one of them. And we may safely believe that he renounced many times in his childhood, for the sake of truth, little advantages which seemed great ones in his eyes, as readily as he was one day to sacrifice an empire to the consistency of his life.

Fig. 4: Bust of Nefertiti (Egyptian Museum of Berlin).

CHAPTER 3

ALONE AGAINST MILLIONS

In about 1352 BC the prince ascended the throne of his fathers as Amenhotep IV, king of Egypt, emperor of all the lands extending from the borders of the Upper Euphrates down to the Fourth Cataract of the Nile—in modern words, from the neighborhood of Armenia to the heart of the Sudan.

He was crowned not at Thebes but at Hermonthis—the "Southern Heliopolis"—where a brother of Queen Tiye was high-priest of the Sun. The list of his titles, as found in the earliest extensive inscription yet known of his reign, presents an interesting combination of the old traditional style with expressions foretelling an entirely new order of thought. It runs as follows:

> Mighty Bull, Lofty of Plumes, Favorite of the Two Goddesses, Great in kingship at Karnak, Golden Horus, Wearer of diadems in the Southern Heliopolis, King of Upper and Lower Egypt, High-priest of Re-Horakhty of the Two Horizons rejoicing in his horizon in his name 'Shu-which-is-in-the-Disk'; Nefer-kheperu-Re, Ua-en-Re; Son of Re; Amenhotep, Divine Ruler of Thebes, Great in duration, Living forever, Beloved of Amun-Re, Lord of Heaven, Ruler of Eternity. (Breasted 1906)

In this long succession of titles, the one of "High-priest of Re-Horakhty of the Two Horizons rejoicing in his horizon in his name 'Shu-which-is-in-the-Disk'" is remarkable. Whatever may be the higher conception of the Sun which the new king was soon to preach, we must remember that originally his God was the Sun-god revered in the old sacred city of Heliopolis (On) and identified with the well-known Re. The Pharaoh never attempted to conceal the identity of his God with the antique solar deity; rather he gave the immemorial deity a new interpretation. The compound name which we have just recalled was therefore but another designation of the god Aten.

Why was that designation specially chosen to figure in the titulary of the newly-crowned Pharaoh? Why not simply the words "High-priest of Aten"? It may be that the compound name, being of more current use, was considered more suitable in an official document. It may be, also, that the king was already conscious that the real God whom he loved was something more subtle than the visible Sun; the expression "Shu" (heat, or heat and light)[1] "which-is-in-the-Disk" rendered the idea of that unknown reality as adequately as language permitted.

One might think that such a consciousness was well-nigh impossible in a boy not yet in his teens. Most writers do, in fact, insist on the king's extreme youth, and seem to believe that the religious views of which we find the evidence in documents dating from this early period of his reign, were mostly, if not entirely, those of the dowager queen and of her entourage.

That Amenhotep IV was a mere child in years, and consequently in worldly experience, is beyond doubt. The letters in which Dushratta (or Tushratta), king of Mitanni, asks him to refer to his mother concerning all matters previously discussed with Amenhotep III, prove that, at least for some time after his accession, he still acted practically as a minor, under the tutelage of Queen Tiye.

It is likely that the messages addressed to him by foreign kings and by vassals were first read by her, and not handed over to him without ample comments about the intentions of their writers, whom she had learnt to know through and through, and to tackle with all the shrewdness of a diplomat. It is possible that certain changes in the dealings of the Egyptian court with foreigners, the reluctance of the young king, for instance, to lavish his gold on his neighbors, in extravagant presents, as his father had done were partly due to the influence of Queen Tiye.

But religious and philosophical matters were quite a different thing. On that plane, as I remarked before, Amenhotep IV, though still a child in years, probably showed signs of an extraordinary power of intuition and of both analytical and creative intelligence far beyond his age. We cannot, it is true, assert on the sole ground of a few words in his titulary that he had already conceived the idea of a God of a more subtle nature than the material Sun. But we can no more reasonably deny him the capacity of conceiving such an idea on the sole ground that he was not more than twelve years old. It is quite possible that it was he himself who insisted on being called, in the list of titles that was soon to remain officially attached to his name, "High-priest of Re-Horakhty" (*i.e.*, of Aten), as other Pharaohs had been called "High-priest of Amun." Moreover, we see that at the present stage of his history, he still bore the name of Amenhotep, and that the most distinctive of all the titles which accompanied his name in later days—that of "Living in Truth" —was not yet mentioned in the inscriptions.

---

[1] Budge (1923: 80).

A KING AND A GOD

We must remember that Sun-worship had never meant to Amenhotep IV what it meant to everybody else. Enraptured, from the very start, by the beauty of light, which seems to have made upon him an extraordinary impression all through his life, he saw in our Parent Star neither a god among many other gods, nor a physical body among many other physical bodies. Rather, it was the supreme source and embodiment of all that appeared to him worth adoring: beauty, power, heavenly majesty—and kindness.

It is likely that he had once associated all the divine attributes of the Sun with the material Disk, but that very soon he had conceived a more subtle idea of the divine by considering the "Heat" or "Heat-and-Light"-(Shu)-which-is-in-the-Disk. The god Re-Horakhty of the Two Horizons of which, in his titulary, he proclaims himself the high-priest, is referred to under that particular name. We should, it seems, suppose that the king's third step was to identify the "Heat within the Disk" with the Disk itself—the invisible form of God with the visible.

All religious geniuses seem to have become aware, in their meditations, of some indefinable oneness, the nature of which it is impossible to convey to those who have not lived through the mystic state. In the case of Amenhotep IV, the truth he was to set as the foundation of his teaching can be expressed today in scientific terms. Originally, the object of his meditations was neither a metaphysical entity, nor an idea, nor a symbol, nor anything abstract, but solely the visible Sun—the father from whom our material earth and its sister planets sprang. Therefore, any discovery concerning Him, through whatever channel it be made, was, in the long run, susceptible of being tested by the ordinary scientific means by which we test all knowledge of the material world.

And, as Petrie (1904: 214) has admirably pointed out, the young Pharaoh's discovery of the equivalence of light and heat, and of the Sun as source of all power has been tested in recent times, and proved accurate. It is nothing else but an anticipation of the principle of equivalence of all forms of energy, which is the basis of modern science. If so, we may regard his identification of Aten with Re-Horakhty of the Two Horizons, rejoicing in His name, "Shu (heat, or heat and light)-which-is-in-the-Aten," as an equally bold anticipation of the fundamental identity of "energy" with what appears to the senses as "matter."

In other words, Amenhotep IV reached, through some direct realization of the essence of all things, the ultimate result that scientific thought was one day to attain, after 33 centuries of patient labor. Whether such occurrences as fits or trances helped him to leap into supernormal stages of consciousness, or whether he reached those stages simply through an unusual aptitude for concentrated meditation, it makes little difference. The fact that, by sole means of direct insight, he grasped the fundamental truth concerning the material no less than the spiritual world, and opened to himself the only outlook on nature and on divinity which can be called scientific in all times, is perhaps the most illustrative historic proof of the unity of all truth.

EARLY DAYS OF THE REIGN OF LIGHT

The Pharaoh's first important act of which there is any record was the erection in Thebes of a temple to Aten. Like all the buildings consecrated to the Disk, that temple was utterly destroyed in subsequent years by the enemies of the king's faith, and nothing is left of it save a few blocks of sandstone, detached from one another, which were mostly re-used in the construction of later monuments. It appears to have been a large building, if we judge by the size of the fragments of bas-reliefs that can still be seen on some of the blocks. An inscription states that new quarries were opened at Silsileh, in the South, to provide sandstone for the construction of this temple. High officials of the court were appointed to supervise the transport of the stone to Thebes. We also know from an inscription that a scribe named Hatay was made "overseer of the granaries in the House of Aten."

From the little that remains of it, it is hardly possible to tell whether the temple was built in the traditional style or whether it resembled the temples of Tell-el-Amarna, of which we shall speak later on. In the writing upon the stones that belonged to the new building, as well as in the well-known inscription of Silsileh, the king is referred to as Amenhotep, which shows that he had not yet changed his name. The name of Aten is not surrounded by a "cartouche," as it is in all later inscriptions. Moreover, references to several of the gods recognized by orthodox Egyptians—such as Horus, Set, Wepwat—are to be read upon the fragments of stone that once formed the temple walls.

Apart from that, above the commemorative inscription of Silsileh, there was originally a figure of the king praying to Amun while the Sun-disk with rays ending in hands—the distinctive symbol of the new religion—shed its life-giving beams upon him. The image of the national deity has been afterwards effaced; but traces of it are still visible. In the tomb of Ramose, in Thebes, which dates from about the same time apparently, there is an image of the goddess Maat. And, in a letter addressed to the king in the fifth year of his reign, by a royal steward named Apiy, who lived in Memphis, Ptah and "the gods and goddesses of Memphis" are mentioned without Apiy seeming to suspect in the least that his sovereign no longer adhered to the traditional religion—an instance all the more impressing that here, in that letter, Amenhotep IV is for the first time referred to as "Living in Truth," the motto which he kept to the very end of his reign. Finally, on the scarabs of this period, the Pharaoh is spoken of as "beloved of Thoth," the god of wisdom.

From these various data, most authors have inferred that, when he built this first temple to Aten of which history tells us, the king had not yet conceived his religion in its definitive form. This interpretation presupposes that the changing of the king's name, the abolition of all cults save that of the imageless Aten, the erasure of the name and figure of Amun and the plural word "gods" from every stone, were all unavoidable consequences of the new faith. And it is generally in that light that those facts are viewed.

It has been written that Aten was "a jealous god,"[2] as if the Pharaoh, in waging war upon the gods of his fathers, was but implicitly obeying some rigorous religious dictate similar to the first of the Ten Commandments that Moses was one day to give his wandering Israelites. Perhaps a certain resemblance between one of the king's hymns to the Sun and Psalm 104, written centuries later; perhaps, also, some unconscious desire of seeing in Amenhotep IV the forerunner of a religion out of which Christianity was one day to spring, has prompted many modern authors to attribute to him a monotheism of the same nature as that of the Jews.[3] The data concerning the construction of the earliest temple to Aten, and the whole of the monarch's reign up to his sixth year, do not point to such a religious conception. Therefore the writers conclude that the king did not know his own mind before the sixth year of his reign, or at least that his faith evolved after that period in the sense of a more and more rigorous monotheism.

But, to a man with no preconceived idea whatsoever as to what sort of a god Aten should be, it does not appear at all necessary to suppose anything of the kind. For if, indeed, as Petrie (1904: 214) has pointed out, Aten be none other but radiant energy deified—that is to say, an all-pervading reality of an immanent character—there is no reason to attribute to Him the all-too-human desire of being worshipped alone. On the contrary, it would seem natural that one who sees divinity in the "Heat-which-is-in-the-Disk," far from proscribing the time-honored gods of his land, should look upon them as man's halting attempts to reach the unreachable. In other words, as imperfect symbols of the one true God. It is thus that sages of all times have looked upon the traditional deities in lands where popular polytheism prevails side by side with the most exalted religious realizations.

And it seems to us most probable that Amenhotep IV considered the gods of his country in that very light. It may be that the figure of Amun was carved out on the slab bearing the Silsileh inscription by a sculptor who "simply fol-

---

[2] See Petrie (1924: 95), Weigall (1922: 168-170; 1923: 82), and Baikie (1926: 251).
[3] It has been asserted that Jewish Monotheism was entirely derived from the worship of Aten. See Freud's *Moses and Monotheism* (1939). See also Weigall (1923: 93).

lowed the time-honored custom" (Baikie 1926: 254). But, had the king found the slightest objection to its presence, he would certainly have had it effaced—as he did, in fact, later on.

The thing is that he had no quarrel with any of the gods, not even with Amun. His God was above them all and contained them all as He contained all existence. At most, the king may have felt a little contempt for the man-made deities, on account of their local character and of their alleged petty interferences in human affairs. He did not love them. But, at first, he tolerated them, knowing that most men can never rise to a higher and more comprehensive idea of divinity.

It seems that he would easily have tolerated them to the end, had it not been for the serious opposition of the Egyptian priests—especially of those of Amun—to the execution of his legitimate designs. The series of steps he was soon to take, and the new aspect of his religion in the eyes of whoever considers it from outside, can be explained as a masterful reaction to unwelcome priestly interference rather than as signs of a religious evolution towards a new and narrower idea of God. This view receives confirmation from the fact that, even after the abolition of the public cult of Amun and of the other gods, still the Pharaoh made no attempt to spread his own faith beyond a small circle of disciples.

THEBES: "BRIGHTNESS OF THE ATEN"

It is also supported by the inscription in the tomb of Ramose at Thebes. The general tone of the inscription plainly indicates that, at the time the tomb was built, not only was the king already in possession of a definite truth which he had received directly from God but that he was, also, fully conscious of being, himself, substantially identical with the essence of all life, the Sun. He addresses himself to Ramose in the inscription, and says:

> The words of Re are before thee, of my august Father who taught me their essence. All that is His…since He equipped the land… in order to exalt me since the time of the god…. It was known in my heart, opened to my face—I understood. [And Ramose answers:] Thy monuments shall endure like the heavens, for thy duration is that of Aten therein. The existence of thy monuments is like the existence of His designs. Thou hast laid the mountains; their secret chambers. The terror of thee is in the midst of them as the terror of thee is in the hearts of the people; they hearken to thee as the people hearken. (Breasted 1906: 389)

The old Sun-god Re, the divine Ancestor of the most ancient Pharaohs, is clearly regarded here as the same as Aten. But if we bear in mind all that we already know of the religion of Amenhotep IV—his idea of the "Heat-which-is-in-the-Disk" identical with the Disk itself, his conception of a thoroughly immanent God—then we see much more than customary dynastic boasting in the king's assertion that Re is his "august Father."

This document is a further proof that, even in this first part of his reign, the Pharaoh's religious views already appeared to other men as something decidedly new. They probably were very little, if at all, different from what we know them to have been at the time he lived in his new capital and wrote his famous hymns.

The king's next step was to decree that the quarter of Thebes in which the newly-built temple stood would henceforth be called "Brightness of Aten, the Great One." Thebes itself—the proud City of Amun, whose patron-deity had become the god of a whole empire—would henceforth be known as the "City-of-the-Brightness-of-Aten."

One need not see in this a deliberate insult to the local god on the part of Amenhotep IV. There is, at least, no evidence suggesting that such might have been the monarch's intention. And if our interpretation of his religious views be right, there is every reason to believe that it was not so. The Pharaoh did not endeavor to crush the Theban deity out of existence, or even to defy it, as the worshipper of a "jealous god" would have done. He only wished to keep it in its place—to relegate it among the partial symbols of divinity which a man who thinks and feels must sooner or later learn to transcend. He did not suppress the cult of Amun or of any other gods; nor, probably, did he intend to do so at this stage of his career. But he surely wished that the one invisible, intangible God, essence of all things, should be honored above all the minor deities, protectors of families, cities, or even nations, whose power was limited and whose nature was apparently finite. And, in giving its new name to the capital of his fathers, he paid a public homage to the true God of the whole universe, as opposed to all the man-made tribal gods.

It is likely that the priests of Amun failed to understand this attitude. As a result, they were unable to accept the change with equanimity. They and their god had been receiving such extraordinary honors in Thebes and throughout Egypt, for so many centuries, that it was hard for them to realize that a new order was dawning, in which their unchallenged domination would no longer have a meaning, and therefore a place. Amun, whom they had identified with the old Heliopolitan god Re—the Sun—so as to legitimize his sway over all Egypt, was in their eyes the actual sovereign of the land. It was he who had rendered his sons, the Theban Pharaohs, invincible in war, magnificent in peace. And it was the custom that they should visit every day his shrine, and, through the performance of certain traditional rites, receive from him the breath of life—justify, through a daily renewed supply of divine power, their age-old claim to divinity.

We know not at what time Amenhotep IV ceased to conform himself to this practice. But we may conjecture that he did so very early in his reign if, as suggested in the inscription in Ramose's tomb, he already realized that his oneness with the Sun was a fact, and that therefore he needed no rites to maintain it or even to assert it. Doubtless the priests resented bitterly this break with immemorial tradition. What they resented no less—if not more—was the steady decrease in the revenues of their temples, now that the king had started encouraging the sole cult of the Disk, and had withdrawn from them the habitual royal gifts, which were enormous.

We do not know how, nor exactly when, they began to show stern opposition to the Pharaoh's designs. The only record of that opposition is a later inscription in which the king tells of the priest's wickedness. The inscription is mutilated, and the reference therefore vague, though vehement.[4] In all probability, however, the step we just spoke of—the renaming of the City of Amun (Nut-Amun, or Thebes) as the "City-of-the-Brightness-of-Aten"—was the signal of a bitter conflict between the king and the ministers of the Theban god.

It is difficult to say what the priests actually did to assert what they considered to be their god's rights. Did they try to frighten the people by foretelling calamities which they ascribed beforehand to the wrath of the deity? Did they start spreading rumors against the king, in order to create disaffection? Or did they use men in their pay to do more effective mischief—to try, for instance, to destroy the newly-erected temple of Aten, or even to make an attempt on the monarch's life? We shall never know. But they appear to have been capable of anything, once their fanaticism was stirred. And, if we judge by the extreme measures which the king took immediately in reply to their intrigues, we may believe that the servants of Amun and of the other gods acted with unusual harshness towards him who, until then, had tolerated their faith and who, even afterwards, was never to seek to harm their persons.

The outcome of the struggle was a change not in the king's actual religious outlook, but in his practical attitude towards the national forms of worship, and a series of new decrees of an uncompromising spirit, by which all hopes of future reconciliation were annihilated at one stroke. The priests of Amun were dispossessed of their fabulous wealth. The name of Amun and the

---

[4] "For as my Father liveth…more evil are they (the priests) than those things which I have heard in the fourth year; more evil are they than those things which King… heard; more evil are they than those things which Men-kheperu-Re (Thotmose IV) heard…in the mouth of Negroes, in the mouth of any people."—(From a mutilated inscription on one of the boundary-stones of Tell-el-Amarna).

plural word "gods" were erased from every stone where they were found, whether in public monuments or in private tombs. Even the compound proper names which contained that of the Theban god were not allowed to remain. And the Pharaoh did not hesitate to have the name of his own father erased, even from the inscriptions in his tomb, and replaced by one of the other names by which he had been well known: Neb-maat-Re.

And by the sixth, perhaps even the end of the fifth year of his reign, the young king changed his own name from Amenhotep—meaning, as we have seen: "Amun is pleased," or "Amun is at rest"—to Akhenaten—"Joy of the Disk," that is to say, "Joy of the Sun". The cult of Amun, and finally that of the innumerable other national gods and goddesses, was abolished, and images were destroyed.

It is these measures which seem to have stirred the indignation of Akhenaten's modern detractors, and prompted them to call him a "fanatic," an "iconoclast," and so forth. But we believe it would be more in keeping with historical truth to see in them, as I have said, a vigorous reaction against sacerdotal interference, a determined assertion of the Pharaoh's rights, as a ruler, against a class of ambitious men who, under the cover of religion, had been grabbing more and more power for centuries. The man who conceived God as the all-pervading impersonal life-force—the energy within the Sun—cannot have shared the aggressive piety of such later believers as Charlemagne or Mahmud of Ghazni, the Idol-breaker. It is unreasonable—nay, absurd—to attribute to him a zeal of the same nature as theirs.

The only reasonable course before him was that which he took and followed, in fact, to its utmost implications. It was not "religious fanaticism," but a clear understanding of the situation that prompted him to act. The "fanatics" were not he, but the priests. It was they who, by their violent hostility to a teaching of exceedingly broad significance, set forth the dilemma which we have just recalled. The thoroughness with which Akhenaten followed his course is one of the early recorded instances of that unbending determination that he showed all his life, once he felt sure which way he was to act in accordance with truth.

A BUDDING MONISM

In fact, it is not exactly for what one could call religious reasons that the priests of Amun and of the other gods showed such stubborn opposition to the king's projects.

It has been said that "the religious thought of the period just preceding the reign of Akhenaten was distinctly monotheistic in its tendencies" (in Baikie 1926: 314), and that, with all its startling originality, the new movement was the natural outcome of the long unconscious evolution of the Egyptian mind. The universal power of the Sun is already asserted in the famous "Hymn to Amun as he riseth as Horus of the Two Horizons," inscribed upon the stele of the two brothers Hor and Suti, architects of Amenhotep III. He is called there: "Sole Lord, taking captive all lands, every day"—an expression hardly different from that which we find later on in Akhenaten's hymns, and which may well be much older than the inscription quoted. In the same inscription, the name of Aten appears as practically identical with that of Amun, for the "Hymn of Amun" runs: "Hail to thee, O Aten of the day, Thou creator of mortals and maker of their life."[5]

It has even been proved that, under Amenhotep III, a temple to a god bearing the full title of "Horus of the Two Horizons, rejoicing in his horizon in his name 'Shu-(heat)-which-is-in-the-Aten-(Disk)'"—the title we find in Akhenaten's inscriptions—existed, with the sole difference that this god was there represented in the traditional style, with a falcon's head. Both the figure and the title are to be found on one of the blocks re-used by King Horemheb in his pylon at Karnak. And in the royal cartouche can be seen the name of Nefer-kheperu-Re (one of Akhenaten's names) altered from that of Amenhotep III.

The elements of the new faith were therefore, to some extent, latent within the old. What Akhenaten did was to assert that such a conception of divinity as that of the "Heat (or Energy)-within-the-Disk" at once transcended and comprehended all others. And he possibly preferred to worship his God under the older name of Aten—the Disk—so as to point out, as I have said, the identity of the visible Sun and of the heat within it. Ultimately, it was the oneness of the Visible and the Invisible—of Matter and Energy. Religiously speaking, there was no radical antagonism between his pantheistic monism and the popular polytheism of the priests with the underlying monotheistic tendency that burst out, now and then, in its most intellectual aspects.

The truth appears to be that the priests did not really mind Akhenaten going further than any of the former Egyptian thinkers in his conception of the divine. But they cared a good deal when, as a logical result of his new lofty idea of the divine, he decreed that the City of Amun should henceforth be called: City of the Brightness of Aten. When, in other words, he made public his desire to do all he could to urge Egypt and the empire to look upon the cosmic God as God, the other city-gods, national gods, etc., being nothing, if not secondary aspects of Him, to be merged into His infinity. They objected to his purely religious idea of God being given priority over their mainly customary, ritualistic, and therefore national one. The struggle between the king and them was not a struggle between two different religious conceptions, but perhaps the oldest recorded phase of the still enduring age-long conflict

---

[5] See Budge (1923: 49).

between individual inspiration and collective tradition; between real religion and state religion; between the insight of the religious genius and the vested interests of the spiritual shepherds of the crowd.

Budge has criticized Akhenaten in the most violent language for not having upheld the cult of Amun, already popular throughout the Egyptian empire. "None but one half insane," says he, "would have been so blind to facts to attempt to overthrow Amun and his worship, round which the whole of the social life of the country centred" (1923: 78). Hall, apparently for a similar reason, brings also against the enlightened Pharaoh the same accusation of being "half insane" (1936: 268). It is the expression used, in last resort, by most average men, about the spiritual giants whom they hate without knowing why, but in fact because they are incapable of understanding their greatness. It only shows how irredeemably average even learned scholars can be where religious insight is concerned.

The authors of the foolish statements just quoted seem to have entirely missed the meaning of Akhenaten's efforts. If Aten and Amun were but two Egyptian deities like any other, then indeed the exaltation of the former at the expense of the latter could perhaps be interpreted as the whim of a "fanatic." But if Aten be the name given to deified cosmic energy, while Amun, as everyone knows, is the patron-god of Thebes, promoted to the position of a god of all the empire only through the victories of the Theban Dynasty, then the whole perspective changes. One understands how Akhenaten could not look upon the local deity as identical with the ultimate essence of all existence.

He could not do so, because of the close association of Amun with all the limited interests of nation and church—because of his political miracles, his partiality in war, his satisfaction in man-ordained rituals and sacrifices. He could not merge his own religion of the universe into the existing religion of the State; his own intuitive truth of all times into the narrow framework of custom, which had no meaning to him. What he wanted to do, on the contrary, was to have the true religion recognized as State religion—pushing the existing one into the background. And that seems to have been the reason for his giving a new name to the very stronghold of the national cult, the City of Amun. He wanted to start a new tradition—more rational, more scientific, more beautiful, more truly religious—on the basis of his extraordinary individual insight. He sought to raise the State religion of the future to his own level, and to make himself the spiritual head of the nation, to which he would teach how to transcend nationhood. The priests of the nation stood in his way. He brushed them aside—without, however, persecuting them.

RELIGIOUS STRIFE

The struggle between Akhenaten and the priests was to be a deadly one precisely because it was less a conflict of ideas than a conflict of values. Had the quarrel merely been about the attributes of divinity or some other such question, a compromise might have taken place, if not during the king's life, at least after him. His message, even if rejected, would have left some trace in history. With time, Amun, while still continuing to protect Egypt in war and peace, might have taken over some of the more subtle qualities of Aten. But there was no possible compromise between the values that the inspired Individual, Akhenaten, stood for, and those represented by the priests of the deified State. As we shall see later on, it is the practical implications of his teaching that were finally to estrange the Pharaoh from his people, from his age, from the average men of all ages. In the meantime, his conception of religion was, from the start, a greater barrier between him and his contemporaries than the lofty philosophical tenets of his religion.

The priests would have remained content had he paid lip service to tradition—had he, for instance, continued to accept his divinity as a Pharaoh from a daily ceremonial contact with the divine patron of the Pharaonic State, in his temple. It would have mattered little if, while doing so, he worshipped the "Heat-within-the-Disk" as the one supreme reality. But he could not do so. His devotion to the Sun, deeply colored by an artist's emotion, must have had the character of mystic rapture. There was a sort of mysterious understanding, a strange intimacy between the young king and the fiery Disk—something quite different from the official filiations of any prince priding in his solar descent, with any man-made Sun-god. Whether stretching out his hands in praise to the rising or setting Sun, or gazing during the middle of the day into the cloudless abyss which He filled with burning light, Akhenaten was in tune with something intangible, shapeless, unnameable, and yet undeniably real. Something that was, at the same time, within the vibrating waves of existence all round him, within the deep rhythmic life of his body, within the silence of his soul. He experienced his oneness with the Sun, and through Him, with all that is.

This experience made him, in fact, what other Pharaohs were merely by name and by tradition: the true Son of the Sun. What need had he of receiving his divinity from the patron-god of the State, when he was conscious of sharing by nature the life of the real Sun—of being in tune with the essence of all things?

> The heat of Aten gave him life and maintained it in him, and whilst that was in him, Aten was in him. The life of Aten was his life, and his life was Aten's life, and therefore he was Aten. ... His spiritual arrogance made him believe that he was an incarna-

tion of Aten—that he was God; not merely a god, or one of the gods of Egypt—and that his acts were divine. (Budge 1923: 82)

Budge is right, with the difference that there was no "spiritual arrogance" on the part of Akhenaten. The successive stages of consciousness which his detractor ascribes to him, are nothing more than those reached by all men who have the privilege to go through the ultimate religious experience, and who are bold enough to draw to the end the conclusions that it implies. Unknowingly, and also unwillingly, Budge only proves that Akhenaten was a genuine spiritual genius at the same time as an intellectual one, the greatest tribute which a man—and especially a detractor—can pay to another man.

The king's contemporary enemies, apparently, did not understand him any better than his 20th-century critics. Deeply attached as they were to their ideology of dynastic Sun-worship, they could hardly imagine what was going on in the monarch's consciousness. They opposed him for the new values he set forth. They did not even share with him that which enemies often hold in common: an ultimate similarity of purpose if not of views.

The people, who doubtless considered their Pharaoh in the same light as their fathers had done, must have been at a loss to make sense of what appeared to them as meaningless, sacrilegious novelties.

I doubt if even Akhenaten's followers—and they appear to have been numerous in the beginning—were able to grasp the full significance of his message. The inscriptions which some of the most prominent of them have left in their tombs, at Tell-el-Amarna, tend to point out that many did not. Most of them seem to have joined the Religion of the Disk for motives either of material interest or of personal attachment to the king—perhaps sometimes for both. It is possible that Akhenaten saw through their minds but accepted their allegiance all the same, hoping, with the natural confidence of youth, to make them sooner or later his true disciples. Yet he had probably already found out how difficult it is to create higher aspirations in men who do not have them, and one may believe that he was not totally ignorant of the enormity of the task before him. He must have realized the strength of tradition, the inborn apathy of the human herd, the frequent incomprehension even of the best intentioned of friends; and, at times, he must have felt desperately alone.

Each time he threw a glance across Thebes from the flat roof of his palace; each time he passed through the streets in his chariot, it certainly struck him how little the capital was worthy of its new lofty name: "City-of-the-Brightness-of-Aten."

The great temple of Amun towered above all the buildings of the immense city. It was now closed by the king's orders. Its splendid halls were silent. And the name of the god had been erased from every pillar, from every wall, from every statue, whether inscribed upon granite or alabaster, or bronze, or lapis lazuli. Still, there it stood, in all its defiant grandeur. It had taken a hundred years to build; a thousand years to adorn, to enrich, to complete. Forty generations of kings had lavished upon it the wealth of the Nile, the treasures of conquered lands, the workmanship of the best artists from all the known world, and had made it a thing unsurpassed in magnificence.

The people bowed down before the closed gates to the hidden deity whom they still revered and feared. The temple remained the heart of Thebes. And there were shrines to other gods within its sacred enclosure—to Mut, Amun's consort; to Khonsu, the Moon-god; to Ptah; to Min—and other temples, all over the city. Every house, in fact, was a temple in which the traditional gods and goddesses were honored daily, and propitiated occasionally, with magic incantations and ritual offerings.

Akhenaten gazed at it all in a bird's-eye view, and understood that Thebes would never be his. What could he do? Destroy all those temples of the man-made gods? He could have done it if he liked. His word was law. And it was not more difficult for him to pull down Karnak stone by stone than to have the name of Amun erased from his own father's tomb. But the idea seems never to have occurred to him. In spite of the hasty judgments passed on him by so many modern critics, he was not an iconoclast. He was too much of an artist ever to dream of becoming one.

He gazed at the sober, majestic architecture of Amun's dwelling-place, and was impressed by its beauty. Then he gazed at the sky—the simple blue depth, without a line, without a spot, without a shade; the void, luminous, fathomless abyss; the dwelling-place of the real Sun in front of which all the splendors and uglinesses of the earth seem equally to vanish into nothingness. And the well-known feeling of absorption into the vibrating infinity, of oneness with that intangible existence that contains all existence, would take him over once more. If only he could have made people understand what he knew, he would not have needed to take steps against the traditional cults. The man-made gods would have automatically sunk into their place as mere symbols, far below the one reality.

But at the sight of the magnificent City of Amun stretched before him, with its temples, its pylons, its avenues bordered with great rams of granite, he knew that he could not. These dazzling earthly glories, with their all-powerful collective associations, would always mean more to the people and the priests than the transparent truth, unconnected with national pride, hopes, or fears, which he had come to realize and to reveal. And no matter how brilliantly and how long he would preach to its thousands the message of the One God made manifest in the real Sun, Thebes would never follow him.

The men of the capital represented that intellectually lazy, superficially artistic, prejudiced, irresponsible, apathetic, uninteresting crowd upon whose stupidity governments and priesthoods are established. Perhaps, indeed, the city-gods that they made so much of were good enough for them. Perhaps any new god they would start worshipping would finally become to them a city-god hardly any better than the old ones. Perhaps gorgeous architectural structures of polished granite and gold would always represent the supreme acquisitions that nations take pride in, and live for, and die for.

But he could not be content with improving on those, as his fathers had. He had raised his senses from the fascination of sculptured curbs and painted colors and resounding formulas, to the inner vision of intangible waves of heat and light. James Breasted has most appropriately called him "the first individual in human history." He was indeed the oldest historic embodiment of the Individual who, in his own singular logic and beauty, stands alone against the background of all times and all countries, in tune with absolute realities and absolute standards forever inaccessible to the many.

Thebes would never side with him. And yet, in his youthful desire for success, in his inherited consciousness of unchecked power, he wished to be a leader. He wished to proclaim far and wide the truth that was to him as clear as daylight, and make the cult of intangible Energy the official State religion of Egypt and of the empire. And he hoped to spread it still further, if possible. He needed the collaboration of men for that great purpose.

And if Thebes was not the place where the first seeds of truth could be sown, there would perhaps be, somewhere down the Nile, an out-of-the-way spot where a new city could be founded—a city, the capital of a new State, which one day, possibly, could become the model of a new world. He would build that ideal State with the help of the few who, if they did not always understand him to perfection, at least seemed to love him. The cult of the One impersonal God would prevail there, and the standards of the enlightened few would be the official standards. The name of Amun and all it stood for would be unknown there from the start.

Thus Akhenaten decided to leave Thebes for good, and to build himself a new capital.

PART II:

THE RELIGION OF THE DISK

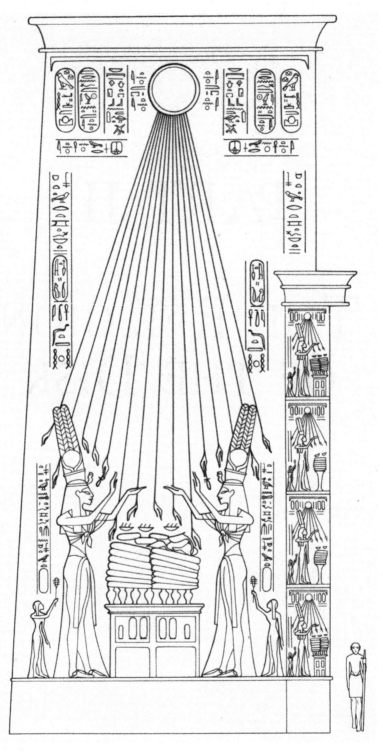

Fig. 5: Reconstruction of a collonade at the Ben-ben shrine.

CHAPTER 4

THE CITY OF GOD

In the sixth year of his reign—that is to say, when he was about seventeen or eighteen—Akhenaten sailed down the Nile to a place some 190 miles from the site of modern Cairo. There he laid there the foundations of his new capital, Akhet-aten—the city of the Horizon of Aten—of which the ruins are known today by the name of Tell-el-Amarna.

He selected, on the eastern bank of the river, a spot where the limestone hills of the desert suddenly recede, enclosing a beautiful crescent-shaped bay, some three miles wide and five miles long. There is a little island in the middle of the Nile, just opposite. The place was lovely. Moreover, it was entirely free from religious or historic associations. In the very words of the king, it belonged "neither to a god nor to a goddess; neither to a prince nor to a princess."[1] And he decided to build upon that virgin soil the city of his dreams.

The city was to occupy part of a sacred territory extending on both sides of the Nile "from the eastern hills to the western hills," an area measuring roughly eight miles by 17. According to an inscription, the king appeared in stately pomp upon a great chariot of electrum drawn by a span of horses.

> He was like Aten when He rises from the eastern horizon and fills the Two Lands with His love. And he started a goodly course to the city of the Horizon of Aten on this, the first occasion…to dedicate it as a monument to Aten, even as his father, Re-Horakhty-Aten, had given command. And he caused a great sacrifice to be offered.[2]

After the customary offerings of food and drink, gold, incense and sweet-smelling flowers, Akhenaten proceeded successively to the south and to the north, and halted at the limits of the territory he wished to consecrate. And he swore a great oath that he would not extend the territory of the city beyond those limits.

---

[1] "First foundation inscription", in Weigall (1922: 84).
[2] "Second foundation inscription", in Weigall (1922: 88).

Akhet-aten was not only to be the new capital of Egypt, but the main centre from which the cult of Aten would radiate far and wide—to the four ever-receding horizons north, south, east and west—and the model, on a small scale, of what the world at large would be if only the spirit of the new rational solar religion would prevail; an ideal abode of peace, beauty, of truth—the city of God. Akhenaten would make it as splendid as he could in the short time it would take him to build it, and continue to adorn it afterwards as long as he lived. And he founded at least two other cities, of lesser proportions and less sumptuous than Akhet-aten, but destined in his mind to be, like it, radiating "seats of truth": one in Syria, of which the name and exact location are unknown; and one in Nubia, on the eastern bank of the Nile, somewhere near the Third Cataract, which he named Gem-Aten, like the temple he had first built in Thebes.

This fact is sufficient to show that, at least as early as the foundation of the city of the Horizon of Aten, in the sixth year of his reign, Akhenaten consciously endeavored to spread the lofty cult of Cosmic Energy to all his empire, if he did not already dream of preaching it beyond the limits of Egyptian civilization. The domain of a universal God could logically admit of no boundaries. And the solemn consecration of the territory of Akhet-aten with all it contained and would ever contain from cliff to cliff, and of at least two similar holy cities, one at each end of his dominions, may be taken as a ritual act symbolizing the Pharaoh's ultimate intention of consecrating the whole earth to the life-giving Sun, its father and sustainer.

THE NEW CENTER OF THE UNIVERSE

According to the inscriptions upon the boundary-stones, the demarcation of the territory of Akhet-aten took place "on the 13th day of the 4th month of the 2nd season," in the sixth year of Akhenaten's reign. The king then returned to Thebes, where he lived until his new capital was inhabitable.

The time between the sixth and the eighth year was spent in preparations. At the Pharaoh's command, hundreds of diggers and bricklayers, masons, carpenters, painters, sculptors, craftsman and artists of all sorts flocked to the site of the new capital. Stone quarries were opened in the neighborhood, while Bek, "Chief of the sculptors on the great monuments of the king," was sent to the south for red granite. Marble and alabaster, granite of different colors, ivory, gold and lapis lazuli, and cedar and various kinds of precious woods were brought from Upper Egypt and from Nubia, from Sinai and Syria, and even further still. The whole empire contributed to the great work undertaken for the glory of the universal God.

And the miracle took place. Within two years or so, temples, palaces, villas, cottages, gardens, lakes full of lotus-flowers, avenues bordered with lofty palm-trees sprang forth from the barren sands. Limited on the east by the desert and on the west by a strip of cultivated land, a mile wide, along the Nile, the town was generally about three-quarters of a mile in breadth, though it stretched over a distance of five miles from north to south. It was, therefore, definitely smaller than Thebes. But it was lovely. It had broad streets, "parks in which were kiosks, colonnaded pavilions and artificial lakes," and plenty of open spaces, shady groves and flowers. Its great temple of Aten was a magnificent building. Its lesser temples, its shrines erected to the memory of the Pharaoh's ancestors, could stand in parallel with any of the most beautiful religious monuments of Egypt; and the king's new palace exceeded in splendor that of his parents in Thebes. And not only were the most costly materials thrown lavishly into the construction of the sacred capital, but "the whole place was planned with delicate taste and supreme elegance."[3]

The main temple of Aten and the king's palace lay in the northern part of the city. Beautiful pleasure-gardens with several artificial lakes—the "Precincts of Aten"—lay to the south. In the white cliffs of the desert that closed the landscape towards the east, were soon to be hewn tombs of the king, royal family and courtiers.

I have already alluded to the existence in architecture, sculpture, painting, and every form of art, of a new style of which the canons, as far as we can infer, may have influenced the decoration even of the earliest temple of Aten, in Thebes. That art, inspired and encouraged by Akhenaten himself, found its everlasting expression in the monuments, the wall-paintings, the statues of Akhet-aten; especially in the great temple of Aten, in the decoration of the king's palace and of the tombs in the eastern hills, and in the beautiful portrait-busts of the Pharaoh and of his queen which rank among the masterpieces of Egyptian sculpture.

In architecture, the break from tradition was perhaps less apparent at first sight than in the other arts. The temples, in Akhet-aten, seen from outside, looked much like the classical Egyptian shrines of the time. When, for instance, after crossing its walled enclosure, one beheld the imposing facade of the great temple of Aten—a pillared portico behind which towered two huge pylons—one had probably the impression of entering a sacred building not much different from those erected in honor of the old gods in the city of Amun. The same five tall flag-staves, from the tops of which fluttered long crimson pennons, shot up against the deep blue sky above each pylon. The same monumental gateway formed the entrance of the temple proper. It was only after its shining doors had been flung open that the difference became evident. One found oneself in a broad paved courtyard flooded with sunshine, in the midst of which stood a high altar on a flight of steps. On either side there was a series of small chapels, brightly decorated.

---

[3] Weigall (1934: 151).

Then, a second gateway led into a second open court, from which one passed into a third, and then into a fourth one, half-filled with a magnificent pillared gallery. The columns were tall and thick enough to give that impression of greatness enduring for ever that one had in Karnak, but from their midst the open part of the court and the blazing sky above could always be seen. The rays of the Disk fell directly upon the golden hieroglyphics in praise of divine light and heat. The cool airy shade made the outer wall appear, by contrast, more luminous and the colored paintings more bright under the dazzling midday Sun. From there, one passed into a fifth, a sixth, and finally a seventh court—all opened to the sky. The two last ones, surrounded by small chapels, had, like the first, an altar in their centre.

There was there nothing of the mystery and sacred awe that generally filled the temples of the traditional gods. There were no dimly-lit lamps hanging from gloomy ceilings; no precious images buried in the depth of pitch-dark sanctuaries like stolen treasures in a cave. There was no gradual passage from sunshine to shade, from shade to gloom, from gloom to complete darkness—the abode of an awe-inspiring hidden god. But a visit to the temple, even to the innermost altar, was but a natural transition from the all-pervading radiance of the fiery Disk, from the blazing heat of the world vivified by His beams, to the worship of the unknown invisible essence behind that light, behind that heat—of the power, of the Soul of the Sun.

At different times of the day, bread and wine and frankincense and beautiful flowers were offered upon the altars to that invisible God whose only image and symbol—the Sun—shone far above, the same in the temple and outside. And clouds of perfume, and waves of music went up to Him and disappeared, dissolved in the golden light of heaven. One was in presence of an entirely new cult; of an entirely new spirit.

Behind the great temple and within the same enclosure there was a smaller one, also faced by a pillared portico. On either side of its entrance, in front of each row of columns, stood a statue of the king and queen. There were shrines all over the city, among which four at least were dedicated to the Pharaoh's ancestors—one to his father, one to his grandfather, Thotmose IV, one to his great-grandfather, Amenhotep II, and one to the father of the latter, Thotmose III. We may suppose that there were more. For it is difficult to believe that Akhenaten would have honored those particular ancestors of his without giving a place in his veneration to his remote predecessors of the Fourth and Fifth Dynasties, the Pyramid builders, in whose days the antique god Re, and the usurper Amun, was the supreme god of Egypt and the sole patron of its divine kings, and whose contemporary art, as we shall soon see, seems to have influenced many of the traits of his own "new style."

As time passed new temples were built. Big or small, they were all built in the same manner, with bright open courtyards and altars covered only by the sky. They were beautifully adorned with paintings and reliefs and statues, generally representing the royal couple (often the royal family) in the act of worship. They had nothing of the ostentatious austerity of a Presbyterian church. But there was in them no idol of any sort to be considered as the receptacle of God. The one symbol of the Religion of the Disk—the Sun, with downward rays ending in hands—appeared repeatedly in the pictures and on the reliefs. But it was there only to remind the worshipper that none but the unseen power within the Sun, the force symbolized by those "hands," was worthy of adoration, and to tell him that no form, however perfect, could ever represent it.

A GLORIOUS CAPITAL

There were beautiful gardens to the south of the city. Cart-loads of good black earth had been brought up from the banks of the Nile and spread out in thick layers over the barren desert. Canals and artificial lakes kept it for ever moist, and beds of flowers destined to exhale their fragrance as a permanent offering to the Sun, and trees both indigenous and foreign, destined to praise Him by their very loveliness, were planted there. The dry, yellow sands gave way to a paradise of fresh perfumes, of beauty and peace. Stumps and roots of trees and shrubs, and withered remains of water-lilies which once rested their large flat leaves and open flowers upon the surface of the lakes, have been discovered by modern excavators.

The whole city was built in the same spirit. It was a place where the enjoyment of the greatest material magnificence was to be allied with a full sense of seriousness—nay, of the sacredness—of life; with the consciousness of the highest spiritual values.

Akhenaten was probably not ignorant of the difficulty of maintaining pace with one's times in the spiritual sphere. As we have seen, he was himself the child of an age of splendor, the scion of centuries of grand material achievements—the flower of Egypt and, one may add, of the whole Near East at the pinnacle of civilization. He knew too well what depths of superstition, what ignorance of the very meaning of spiritual life went along with that worldly wealth and greatness. Whatever was precious in the traditional wisdom of the Egyptians belonged to an earlier and simpler age. And there are signs that seem to indicate that the young Pharaoh, to some extent, wished to revive an age-old cult—namely, the solar cult which had once thrived in the city of Heliopolis—of which the sense had been long forgotten.

But however much the corruption of his brilliant times impressed him, he was too logical not to dissociate in his mind material comfort, beauty, luxury, etc., from the moral coarseness that so often accompanies them. It was diffi-cult to see the two sides of life flourish simultaneously. But there was no reason why they should not do so. Indeed, something told him that they should do so; that, as long as man has a visible body and lives on the material plane, there is no perfection unless they do thrive harmoniously. Himself a living example of opposite qualities admirably balanced, a man in whom, by nature, there was no excess, he wanted the whole of life—material, social, emotional, intellectual—to be a thing of beauty, religious life being the bloom and culmi-nation of it all. He did not believe that wisdom lay in suppressing the natural cravings for worldly comfort and enjoyment, but rather in satisfying them, if possible, and at the same time in purifying them; in living intensely, but with innocence and serenity; in feeling the lovely sensuous objects of this transient world—forms and colors, songs and caresses, the taste of good wine in a finely chiseled cup—the higher realities that these things merely foreshadow and symbolize.

The amulets found in the laborers' rooms, and many a figure on the walls, show distinctly that the worship of the immemorial popular gods and god-desses was predominant among the humble folk, even within the sacred terri-tory specially dedicated to the One Lord of all beings, Aten. The king, so eager to prohibit the public cults of Amun and of the many deities, to have their tem-ples closed and the plural word "gods" effaced from every inscription, seems never to have tried to bring the commoners to abandon their traditional beliefs.

One reason for that apparent indifference may well be that, as I have sug-gested in the preceding chapter, the founder of the Religion of the Disk was much less of a staunch monotheist, in the narrow sense of the word, than both his modern admirers and detractors seem to think. He certainly himself believed in one God alone—one impersonal God, the essence of all existence, personified in the father of all life on our earth, the Sun—but he probably did not object to other people paying homage to deities of a more finite nature, as long as they did so sincerely and in a truly religious spirit. He had dispos-sessed and dismissed the priests who encouraged superstition in view of their own worldly ends and who strongly opposed his cherished plans of making the cult of the one God the State religion of Egypt. He had no quarrel either with the ignorant people or with their childish beliefs. Those beliefs, they would perhaps themselves outgrow with time, provided they could keep their hearts open to the beauty of the sunlit world and their minds receptive to the evidence of truth—provided they could feel and think. In the meantime, it mattered little what names and shapes they held sacred, by custom, as long as their beliefs led them to do no harm. We shall discuss later on the implications of Akhenaten's famous motto, "Living in Truth," but we can already safely say here that he seems always to have valued right living above anything else in a man. For one to live rightly, one's sub-conscious mind, at least—one's deeper self—has to grasp the truth, even if one's conscious mind, blinded by external influences, denies it. And in the eyes of a lover of truth, and of a man of extraordinary intuition as Akhenaten was, it was surely the deeper self that mattered.

Another reason why the Pharaoh appears never to have tried to spread his religion among the commoners was perhaps that he felt it useless to force upon them a simple yet high philosophy which they would not understand, which they were not prepared to live up to, and which they would soon distort. It was far more reasonable to increase their material well-being, so that they might begin to acquire that preliminary sense of the beauty of life, without which the Religion of the Disk loses all meaning; to give them a minimum of comfort and a minimum of leisure, that they might learn the pleasure of letting their eyes wander over an open landscape, while relaxed.

AN ARTISTIC RENAISSANCE

The new movement in art inaugurated by Akhenaten found another masterful expression in the decoration of the royal palace and of the villas of the nobles. Never had Egyptian art been so true to life before, and never was it again to be so after Akhenaten's reign. It was more than a new technique—movement rendered, along with color; expression stressed even above perfection of form—it was a profession of faith. It was the Religion of the Disk made vivid to the senses.

Apart from the information they give about the life of the king and courtiers, the paintings and reliefs in the tombs in the "eastern hills" are, along with the famous portrait-heads found in the studio of several artists in the city, the most illustrative productions of the "new art" of Akhet-aten.

The conventions which had shackled the artist in his rendering of the human figure—and especially of royal personages—and which had limited the sources of his inspiration, have entirely disappeared in the new school. Here we find the Pharaoh and his queen portrayed in all the familiar attitudes of private life—eating, drinking, chatting, smelling flowers, playing with their children, etc.—with a naturalness never attained in Egyptian art before the "Tell-el-Amarna period," and never surpassed in any art. And that is not all: more than one of those pictures and sculptures even present a definite exaggeration of certain features, both of the head and body, which sets them apart from nearly all the productions of the ancient world, and renders them somewhat akin to our modern "futurist" art in its strange aspects. One has only to look at some of the reliefs representing the king himself with an unusually developed skull, a protruding chin, and hips and thighs out of proportion with his slender body. One has only to think of the otherwise beautiful limestone head of one of the princesses in the Cairo museum, whose skull is elongated to an incredible extent, to be convinced of the existence of such a tendency among the artists of Akhenaten's school.

Some modern authors have endeavored to present those strange features as the faithful reproduction of an ungainly countenance, by sculptors and painters trained by the king "living in truth" never to flatter their models, least of all himself and his family.[4] But this view is contradicted by the existence of other portraits of the king and of the princesses—paintings, busts, and statues—in which none of these deformities are to be seen. There is the quartz head of one of the Pharaoh's little daughters at the museum of the Louvre, the head of a normal child of exquisite delicacy. There is the delightful painted relief picturing Akhenaten in his early youth as he smells a bunch of flowers that Nefertiti holds out to him—one of the best productions of the Amarna school; a work which, according to Professor H. R. Hall himself, possesses already a Hellenic grace, and in which the king's figure "reminds one of a Hermes" and "could hardly have been bettered by a Greek".[5] There is the whole series of portrait-busts that represent Akhenaten not as a boy, but as a man, and that attest beyond doubt that he was lovely to look upon.

Akhenaten's physical appearance has been discussed nearly as often as his religious ideas, and sometimes commented upon with as much bitterness. Inasmuch as a body is the reflection of the soul that animates it—or the soul the projection of the body—it is not superfluous to try to visualize him as he once could be seen, when he trod the painted pavements of his palace. From his remains we know that he was a man of medium height; from pictorial evidence, we know that he had a regular oval face, a straight nose, thick, well-designed lips; and that his jet-black eyes were, in the words of Weigall (1922: 52), "eloquent of dreams." He had a long graceful neck, well-shaped arms and legs, and beautiful hands. His body, of which the top part is generally represented bare in the paintings and bas-reliefs, was neither stout nor thin. The pleated cloth he wore wrapped around the hips and tightly tied below the navel, seems to be responsible for the "protruding paunch" to which so many authors allude in their description of him. He has been depicted as having little of a virile appearance and, at first sight at least, this remark is not entirely without grounds.

There was surely an indefinable charm all about his person; a gracefulness of deportment, an irresistible gentleness—something subtly feminine. But at the same time, in those large, dark, loving eyes, whose mere glance was like a caress, one could read courage, determination, a manly depth of thought and

---

[4] See for example Hall (1936: 304); Budge (1923: 103); Baikie (1926: 294).

[5] Hall (1936: 305).

will. Those lips, with their delicate curve, always ready to move into a mysterious smile, expressed the serenity of unshakable strength. There was, in the Pharaoh's countenance, a well-balanced blending of grace, of force, and of poise; of voluptuousness and of character—a living picture of the harmonious plenitude of his being. In other words, Akhenaten seems to have forestalled in real life, to a very great extent, that well-nigh impossible complete human type—young demi-god with the opposite perfections of both man and woman—which Leonardo da Vinci was to conceive and to strive throughout his career to fix in lines and colors, 3,000 years later. And his body, no less than his personality, bore the stamp of that strange dual beauty.

The paintings and sculptures that represent him, or the members of his family, with the exaggerated features I have referred to above, are therefore to be taken not as faithful portraits, but as characteristic instances of a "style." And that "style," apart from any other considerations, contained a religious—perhaps also a political—symbolism. Its productions have no parallel in the immediate past, but they strangely resemble some archaic figures of the Fourth and Fifth Dynasties. Weigall (1922: 64) has given, side by side with the copy of one or two of them, the reproduction of royal heads and of a statuette found by Petrie, the former at Abydos, the latter at Diospolis, and dating as far back as the days of the great pyramid builders. The same receding forehead, protruding chin, elongated skull; the same overstressed hips and thighs are to be remarked in both cases, at a distance of 1800 years or more. So that, indeed, from those quaint samples of the work of the new school of Tell-el-Amarna there is every probability that the distinguished archaeologist is right when he states that

> Akhenaten's art might thus be said to be a kind of renaissance—a return to the classical period of archaic days; the underlying motive of that return being the desire to lay emphasis upon the king's character as a representative of that most ancient of all gods, Re-Horakhty (ibid.: 63).

How closely that aspect of the new art was interwoven with the Religion of the Disk we can only understand after trying to define what place the king occupied in the creed which he preached. It will suffice here to say that the frequency with which those archaic renderings of him and of his family appear in the paintings and sculptures of his time, suggests what stress he himself put upon the great antiquity of his so-called "new" ideas. Akhenaten seems to have shared with many inspired religious leaders the conviction that, far from being an innovator, he was just the expounder of Truth, which is one and of all times, and of which the oldest civilizations had perhaps a more accurate glimpse than the latter ones.

Whatever, in the Amarna School, was not a deliberate attempt at imitating the archaic models, was of utmost grace and naturalness—true to life as never Egyptian art was again to be. We must remember that the young king was the soul of the whole movement:

> It was he who released the artists from convention and bade their hands repeat what their eyes saw; and it was he who directed those eyes to the beauties of nature around them. He and no other taught them to look at the world in the spirit of life; to infuse into the cold stone something of the 'effulgence which comes from Aten.' (Weigall, ibid.: 181)

In the beautiful city I have tried to describe—the dream and the work of one man—life was pleasant. We have already seen what amount of comfort and of freedom the humblest dwellers in the consecrated area enjoyed, in the model settlements built for them near the field of their labors. They probably saw very little of the pomp of the court and, with the exception of those who lived in the city itself, they hardly ever had the opportunity of witnessing the passage of a royal procession. Whether they had or not some sort of vague knowledge of the new creed proclaimed by the king, we cannot tell. They had perhaps heard that he worshipped the Sun alone and despised the other gods; that he was in conflict with the priests of Amun; that he had raised several men of poor extraction to high positions because of their readiness to share his faith; that, in the eyes of his God, Egyptians and foreigners were the same. But, whatever rumors may have reached them in their fields, their factories, or their quarries, that brought no change either in their beliefs or in their lives. As we have seen, they continued to worship in peace the age-old popular deities that they were accustomed to. And the Pharaoh was, to them, what every one of his predecessors had been to the past generations: a divine being, the father and defender of his subjects, the "good god."

If we judge him through the pictures his artists have left of him, Akhenaten was far from being one of those austere thinkers who shun pleasure as an obstacle to the development of the spirit or even as a meaningless waste of time and energy. He seems, on the contrary, to have believed in the value of life in its plenitude, and the paintings that represent him feasting, drinking, listening to sweet music, caressing his wife, or playing with his children, apart from their merit as faithful renderings of everyday realities, had possibly a definite didactic significance. In practically every one of them the lofty symbol of the Religion of the Disk—the Sun with downward rays ending in hands—radiates over the scene depicted, so as to recall the presence of the one invisible reality in the very midst of it. This symbol emphasizes the beauty, the seriousness, nay, the sacredness of all manifestations of life when experienced as they should be, in earnestness and in innocence.

Whether they stand together in adoration before His altar, or lie in each other's arms, the Sun embraces the young king and queen in His fiery emanation; His rays are upon them, holding the symbol *ankh*—life—to their lips. For life is prayer. One who puts all his being in what he feels or does—as he who "lived in truth" surely did—already grasps, through the joyful awareness of his body to beautiful, deep sensations, a super-sensuous, all-pervading secret order, source of beauty, which he may not be in a position to define, but which gives its meaning to the play of the nerves. And he is able above all to acquire, through the glorious exaltation of his senses in love, a positive, though inexpressible knowledge of the eternal rhythm of life—to touch the core of reality.

In allowing a few scenes of his private life to be thus exhibited to the eyes of his followers—and of posterity—was it Akhenaten's deliberate intention to teach us that pleasure, when enjoyed in religious earnestness, transcends itself in a revelation of eternal truth? We shall never know. But one thing can be said for certain, and this is that the instance of that perfect man, on one hand so aware of his oneness with the essence of all things, on the other so beautifully human in his refined *joie de vivre*, is itself a teaching, a whole philosophy. And in him one can see an expounder of precisely that wisdom which our world of today, tired of obsolete lies, is striving to realize, but cannot; a man who lived to the full the life of the body and of the spirit, seriously, innocently, in harmony with the universal principle of light, joy, and fecundity which he worshipped in the Sun. Whether we imagine him burning incense to the majesty of the rising orb, or listening to the love-songs of the day in midst of merriment and enjoying them with the detachment of an artist; whether we think of him entertaining his followers of the marvelous unity of light and heat, 3,300 years before modern science, or abandoning himself to the thrill of human tenderness in a kiss of his loving young queen—the same beauty radiates from his person.

And it is that beauty which, before all, attracts us to him, and, through him, to the Religion of the Disk, that glorious projection of himself in union with the cosmos.

A Blessed Life

As we have just seen, something of Akhenaten's intimate life, perhaps also something of his general philosophy, can be inferred from the pictures that have survived the ruin of his lovely city. Of his inner life, of his thoughts and feelings during those moments of blessed solitude that doubtless followed, with him as with all spiritual geniuses, hours of intense activity, there are no records whatsoever. There cannot be. And yet one feels that nothing would bring one, so as to say, in closer contact with him, than a glance at that particular aspect of his unwritten history.

It is natural to believe that the two hymns that have come down to us—and probably many more, which are lost—were composed by Akhenaten during the hours he was alone. It is therefore, it seems, in the general tone of those poems, as well as in the evocation of the atmosphere in which they were conceived, that one can the best hope to form an idea of the king's mind when away from the crowd of his courtiers and even from the presence of his wife and children—when free from the duties of monarchy, from the obligations of his mission, from the pleasures of love and family life.

The hymns in their details will be discussed later on as the main basis of our knowledge of the Religion of the Disk. But we can already say here, in anticipation of a more complete study of them, that the dominant idea expressed in those songs is that of the beauty of the whole scheme of things as ordained by the Sun—by Him who causes the radiant days to follow the nights full of stars and the seasons to succeed each other. They also contain the belief in an all-pervading, unfailing love, mysteriously inseparable from the energy within the Sun-rays; of a love that gives each speck of life—be it the germ in the bird's egg or the embryo asleep in the depth of a woman's womb—a start on the golden road to full development in health and happiness. They contain the bold certitude of the impartiality of that immanent love, poured out with light and heat, through the life-giving Disk, to all tribes, all nations, all races, all living species, indiscriminately. They assert the unity of life and of the brotherhood of all creatures as a consequence of the universal fatherhood of the Sun.

But remarkably enough for one who would consider those hymns as expressing true facts of nature and nothing more, there is, in them, not the slightest allusion to the dark side of the picture of the world. Not a hint at the millions of cases in which the all-pervading love of the father seems to fail; in which the innocent speck of life—young insect, bird, beast, or baby—is mercilessly crushed before it even had time to know the beauty of light, or grows up only to drag a miserable existence. Not a single word about those cries of distress which, to any sensitive and thoughtful person, so often seem to interrupt the harmony of the universal chorus.

Nobody, with even a superficial knowledge of his life, can suppose in Akhenaten less sensitiveness to suffering, less love for creatures or less intelligence than in the average man. And the only way to explain, therefore, this total omission of all idea of evil from the picture of the universe given in the hymns (at least in the two which we know) is to admit that they were composed during special moments of the king's experience; during moments when the very sight of the world with its incoherent mixture of joy and pain, life and death was lost to him in a state of bliss in which he grasped nothing but the essence of things, retaining of their contradictory appearances those alone that convey the idea of joy and order.

In other words, those poems do express true facts of nature, but at the same time they reveal a plane of consciousness which is not the ordinary plane. They suggest a picture of the world as perceived by one who has transcended the ordinary scale of vision; by one who has reached the stage where he actually feels the inherent goodness and beauty of the whole play of existence behind its transient failures, suffering and death—and ugliness; by one who, above the apparent disorder of phenomenal experience, greets the majesty of everlasting laws, expressions of harmony, glimpses of a reality which is perfect.

Left to himself in the calm of his sumptuous apartments or in the fresh solitude of his gardens, Akhenaten easily raised his soul to that stage of consciousness characterized as bliss in the absence of a more enlightening description of it. Did he reach it systematically, as a result of any physical and mental discipline, or simply as a natural development of his extraordinary sensitiveness, or as the outcome both of a powerful inborn tendency and of willful application? It is very difficult to say; and it matters little.

What is important is that, in all probability, he was familiar with the genuine experience of super-consciousness. It was to that experience that he doubtless owed his astounding insight into scientific truths which could only be proved by the combined intellectual labor of thousands of men, spread over centuries. It seems also certain that, whatever might have been the Pharaoh's deliberate efforts and the inner discipline he underwent, if any, he must have been from the start gifted with powers of intuition out of proportion to those of the ordinary man of science of any age.

He would have developed those powers anyhow. And, with his uncompromising logic as a complement to insight and inspiration; with the absolute sincerity of his nature and the charm of his person, he would still have been, even in a totally different social status, one of the few great men to whom divine honors can be rendered without sacrilege. As things stand, far from having to rise to perfection in spite of his material surroundings, he used a part of the inexhaustible wealth at his command to create for himself, in Akhet-aten, the ideal abode in which he could pass without effort from life in truth and beauty to the contemplation of supreme beauty and supreme truth.

Clad in fine immaculate linen in the midst of those mythical splendors that we can today but faintly recall, the inspired young Pharaoh, half-reclining upon his ivory couch, let his mind drift its natural way. Through a restful perspective of well-shaped pillars, his eyes gazed at a patch of blue sky. Subtle perfumes were floating in the air. The breeze brought him the fragrant breath of flowers. Perhaps the subdued harmony of a distant harp reached him now and then. There was peace all around him—peace in keeping with the silence of his heart and congenial to meditation. The tranquil beauty which his eyes met wherever they looked helped him to forget every possible disturbing thought of imperfection; to detach himself from those appearances which stand in the way of the soul in quest of ultimate truth.

Thus was, as far as we can hope to picture it, the life of the king in Akhet-aten, the city of God, built by him to be an island of peace in this world of strife; to be the model, on a small scale, of what he would have desired the world to become under the beneficent influence of his teaching of truth. We have seen also something of the life of the people there. It was surely not perfect, and Akhenaten knew himself that his new capital, in spite of all his efforts, did not come up to the full expectation of his dream. But it was his dream realized to the extent it could be during the short span of his career, among average men, without the pressure of violent proselytism, without, by the way, any form of creedal proselytism at all among the commoners. It was a beautiful creation.

Fig. 6: Akhenaten and family make an offering to the Aten.

CHAPTER 5

THE WAY OF REASON

As remarks Sir Wallis Budge, it is true that all we know for certain about Akhenaten's teaching is found only in two hymns, one short and one long—the former copied several times, partly or in whole, in different courtier's tombs at Tell-el-Amarna, the latter found written only once on the walls of the tomb of Ay, "fan-bearer on the right side of the King, and Master of the King's House." These two songs in praise of the Sun are all that is left of a probably much more considerable religious literature, the rest having entirely perished in the systematic ruin of Akhet-aten and the persecution of the Religion of the Disk under Tutankhamen and especially under Horemheb.

But I believe that, if one considers the hymns closely, and in the light of all that the reliefs, paintings, and inscriptions tell us about the king's personality and about his life, then one will find that they imply far more than what Budge appears to admit. One will find that the few enthusiastic admirers of the Religion of the Disk, whom the learned but somewhat prejudiced writer criticizes so bitterly, have at least as sound reasons to revere Akhenaten's memory as he himself can have to minimize the young Pharaoh's importance in the history of thought.

The first thing that strikes a modern mind in those very ancient songs is the idea, expressed in them, that the Sun is the ultimate origin to which can be traced all the particular features of our earth, be they meteorological, biological, geographical, or ethnical. To look upon our parent star as the father of all life was not a new thing. Men had done so from the beginning of the world, and this was no doubt the conception at the root of that most ancient and, in former days, most widespread of all religions: Sun-worship. But here, especially in the long hymn, there is something more. Not only is the Sun hailed as the source of all life, but it is He who determines the succession of the seasons; He who causes both the rain to fall in the countries where it rains, and the Nile to overflow Egypt with its life-giving waters; He who is at the back of all differences of climate upon the globe, and subsequently, who is responsible for all differences of color and features, of speech and of diet, among men of various countries.

We must not forget that many of the beliefs which we now regard as "mythology" and treat with the sympathetic smile of grown-up folk for a child's belief in father Christmas, were once held as seriously as other articles of faith are held by our contemporaries. To proclaim, in Eighteenth Dynasty Egypt, that the Nile was a river like all rivers, was to issue a statement about as revolutionary (and shocking) as that of a man who, in medieval Europe, would have openly denied the Christian dogma of the Incarnation. But Akhenaten, like all sincere rationalists, cared little what reactions his beliefs or disbeliefs could start in other people, once he was himself sure that he was in possession of a tangible truth.

We cannot also fail to be impressed by that other idea, namely that the Sun, apart from being the condition and cause of life in general, is the ultimate regulator of each individual life—"setting every one in his place"—and also the differentiator of races and of their characteristics, features, complexion, language, etc., which are finally at the basis of all national feelings among men. In other words, that He is the maker of our globe's history no less than of its geography.

The concept of nation, being closely entangled with a quantity of immediate human interests, is one of those which has been taking the longest time to be viewed objectively. In the days of the apogee of Egypt with which we are here concerned, a nation was that group of people who worshipped the same national gods, and especially who went to battle in the name of the same war-gods. The conception of a "God of all lands" in whose light all those local deities were but magnified men and women was novel enough. The scientific idea that all differences among groups of men were the product of man's physical environment, and that the physical environment was finally conditioned by the climate, that is to say, by the Sun, was amazingly in advance of Akhenaten's times. Far from merely amounting to the exaltation of any particular sun-god, it was the plain, rational assertion that our parent star, origin and regulator of all life on this earth, is ultimately responsible for man's collective creations. In a word, man is, before all, "a solar product."

DIVINE ENERGY: "SHU-WHICH-IS-IN-THE-DISK"

I have just referred to the visible Sun, the flaming Disk in the sky—Aten in the literal sense. And had Akhenaten worshipped nothing more than it, still his religion, with its most scientific view of the earth and of man purely as "solar products" would be something far in advance of most ancient and modern religions based upon dogmatic assumptions that bear little or no relation to elementary physical facts. But there is more in it.

As we have already seen in the preceding chapters, one of the names of the Sun the most widely used by Akhenaten in the inscriptions is "Re-Horakhty of the Two Horizons, rejoicing in His Horizon, in His name 'Shu-which-is-in-the-Disk,'" or "the living Horus of the Two Horizons, rejoicing in

His Horizon in His name 'Shu-which-is-in-the-Disk'"—the name under which both the hymns that have come down to us are addressed to Him.

"Shu," as an ordinary noun, we must translate by "heat" or "heat and light," for the word has these meanings. In the pyramid texts, Shu is the name of a god symbolizing the heat radiating from the body of Tem, the creator of the solar Disk, in the indivisible trinity Tem-Shu-Tefnut—father, son and daughter; the Creator of the Sun-disk, the Heat and the Moisture; the principle of fertility, and its indispensable agents. Whatever be therefore the interpretation we give to the word, we have to admit that "the king deified the heat of the Sun"—or the "heat and light," as Budge himself says—"and worshipped it as the one eternal, creative, fructifying and life-sustaining force."

This permits us to assert with Petrie (1904: 214) that in the Religion of the Disk, the object of worship was "the radiant energy of the Sun," of which heat and light are aspects.

On the other hand, it is true, as Budge says, that "the old Heliopolitan traditions made Tem-Re, or Khepera, the creator of Aten (the Disk), but this view Amenhotep IV rejected, and he asserted that the Disk was self-created and self-subsistent." This statement is all the more significant because it comes from a scholar who, far from being one of Akhenaten's admirers, has never lost an opportunity to minimise the importance of his teaching. Here, the enormous gap between the Religion of the Disk and the old Heliopolitan cult is emphasized without the learned author seeming to suspect what a homage he is paying, indirectly, to the young Pharaoh's genius. For if the object of the latter's adoration were purely "the heat and light," or energy within the Disk, then one fails to understand why he rejected the view of the priests of Heliopolis about a god separate from the Disk and creator of it.

And if, on the contrary, the object of his worship were the material Disk itself and nothing more, then why should he have called it "Shu-which-is-in-the-Disk"? Moreover, why should he say in the short hymn: "At Thy rising, all hands are lifted in adoration of Thy Ka"? And, again, in the long hymn, speaking this time of the worship of the Sun, not by men, but by birds: "The feathered fowl fly about over the marshes, praising Thy Ka with their wings"? In the case of a living being its "Ka" designates its double, or soul; that invisible element of it which survives death; its subtle essence as opposed to its coarser visible body. The "Ka" of the Sun would therefore be the Sun's soul, so to say; the subtle principle which is the essence of the Sun, and which would survive the material Disk, were it one day to decay and pass away—the eternal Sun, as opposed to the visible Sun.

I believe that the best way to account for this apparent ambiguity is to admit that Akhenaten worshipped the radiant energy of the Sun as the principle of all existence on earth, but deliberately brushed aside the Heliopolitan distinction between the god, maker of the solar Disk, and the solar Disk itself. To him there was no such distinction. To him the Disk was self-created and self-sustaining, because it was but a visible manifestation of Something more subtle, invisible, intangible, everlasting—its "Ka" or essence. And Shu, the heat and light, the energy of the Sun, was not the emanation from the body of a god different from it, but the manifestation of that one thing which the visible flaming Disk was another manifestation. It was the Disk itself, and the Disk was it.

Visible matter was not the product of energy, distinct from it, nor energy the product of matter, distinct from it. Nor were any particular forms of energy, such as heat and light, the products of any creative power distinct from them by nature. But, as was to be suggested 3,300 years later by the inquiries of the modern scientists into the structure of the atom, matter and energy were inseparable, and both everlasting; they were one. To maintain the distinctions put forward in olden days by the priests of the Sun in Heliopolis was to deny the secret identity of the visible and invisible Sun, of the visible and invisible world, of energy and matter.

That identity, Akhenaten had become aware of through some mysterious inner experience of which history has not preserved any description, and by which transcended the human to reach the cosmic scale of vision. It is probable that he could not explain it, as the scientists of our age do, in terms of definite patterns of energy. But he knew it, none the less, to be the objective truth. And, anticipating in a tremendous intuition the rational conclusions of modern research, he based his religion upon the three ideas that summarize them, namely:

(1.) The essential *equivalence of all forms of energy*, including that yet today unanalyzed form which is life;

(2.) The essential *identity of matter and energy*, each of the two being but the subtler or the coarser aspect of the other;

(3.) The *indestructible existence*, without beginning, without end, of that one unknown thing, which is matter to the coarser and energy to the finer senses.

A True Visionary

The "Ka" of the Sun, mentioned in the hymns, must indeed be taken to mean the soul or essence of our parent star. And it seems certain that the immediate object to which the king's followers were invited to offer their praise was not the material Disk alone, nor the "Ka" of the Disk regarded as distinct from it, but the Disk with its "Ka," regarded as one.

In the hymns, it is repeatedly stated that Aten is "one" and "alone." It is said, for instance, in the short hymn, "Thou Thyself art alone, but there are millions of powers of life in Thee to make them (Thy creatures) live." And again in the other hymn, "O Thou One God, like unto Whom there is no other, Thou didst create the earth according to Thy heart (or will), Thou alone existing."

It is true that the worshippers of every great god in Egypt had from time immemorial declared that their god was "one" even while they themselves admitted the existence of different gods. We find the expression "one" and "alone" in older anonymous hymns to Amun, to Re, to Tem, and other deities, long before Akhenaten. And it is also true that "it was obvious that Aten, the solar Disk, was one alone and without counterpart or equal" (Budge 1923: 79). But if we see in Akhenaten's identification of the solar Disk with its "Ka" the sign of his belief in the oneness of invisible energy and visible matter, then the words "one" and "alone" become more than casual utterances. They express the only knowable attribute of that supreme entity, substance and power at the same time, which is at the back of all existence. They qualify the essence of all suns—the universal "Ka"—not only the essence of our Sun. For these are the same. And whether Akhenaten personally knew or not of the existence of other suns besides the one that rules the life of our earth, it makes little difference. His religion bears from the start the character of the broadest and most permanent scientific truth, embracing, along with the reality of our solar system, that of all existing systems.

For we know today that the self-same earthly varieties of what we call matter go to compose the visible bodies of all distant worlds in space. We know that the heat and light that our Sun sends us through His beams, the "Shu-within-the-Disk" that Akhenaten adored, is the self-same radiant energy that burns and shines in the remotest nebulae. For us, born after the invention of the telescope and of the spectroscope, the ritual worship of our Sun, coupled with the modern belief in the essential identity of matter and energy, is a symbolical homage. Through Him, the visible Disk, father and mother of the Earth and our sister planets, our adoration goes to that ultimate unknown, father and mother of all the worlds that spin round and round their respective suns, in fathomless infinity; to that ultimate unknown that contains movement, and heat and light, and finally life and consciousness within it: cosmic energy.

To Budge and to many others, it may seem "inconceivable" to attribute to a man born centuries before the invention of the telescope, anything approaching our grandiose vision of millions of suns and planets evolving through the unlimited abyss of interstellar void, in a divine dance without beginning or end. But who can tell how far man's insight can take him, even without the precise intellectual knowledge of its objects? Who can tell if

Akhenaten, gazing at the glory of his clear night sky full of stars, did not conceive the idea that each of those distant lights might well be a Sun, like ours, maker of worlds over which he daily rises and sets? And who can tell how far in Egypt astronomy had actually reached, even without the help of the telescope? Much of it was secret and has been lost. I therefore cannot assert that, in deifying the radiant energy of the Sun and the Disk itself, the inspired youth did not deliberately put forward the worship of that indefinable, unknown, and perhaps unknowable reality that modern science meets both in the atom and in the systems of starry space.

Whatever may have been the limitations imposed upon his knowledge of the physical universe by the technical conditions of scientific investigation in his time, it remains true that the cult which he evolved is that of the only thing which modern science can hail as the ultimate reality—as God, if science is ever able to speak of a God. It matters little whether he could or could not appreciate his own creation from the point of view of a modern scientist, even from that of a layman of today with a summary knowledge of the conclusions of science. And if one suggests that this was impossible, then all one can say is that the relation of his religion to the great facts of physical existence, discovered millennia after him, is all the more admirable, and his genius all the more staggering.

A METAPHYSICS OF LIGHT

The only materials on which we can base our knowledge of the Religion of the Disk are too scanty for us to be able to say how far its founder was aware of the structure of the physical universe as we have learnt to conceive it. It is interesting, however, to consider how exactly certain of Akhenaten's main utterances tally with those conclusions of modern thought now looked upon as definite *scientific* acquisitions.

One of the points on which he insists the most, in both of the hymns which have survived, is the all-importance of the beams of the Sun. Not only does he say: "Thou sendest forth Thy beams and every land is in festival," but also: "Breath of life is to see Thy beams," and also: "Thy beams envelop (*i.e.*, penetrate) everywhere, all the lands which Thou hast made"... "Thou art afar off, but Thy beams are upon the earth"; and again: "The fishes in the river swim up to greet Thee; Thy beams are within the depth of the great sea..."

The rays of the Sun play an equally prominent part in the symbol of Akhenaten's religion: the Disk with downward beams ending in hands which hold the looped-cross *ankh*, sign of life. No other image but that one was allowed in the temples, and that was not intended to portray the object of worship, but to remind the worshippers of the main truth concerning it—the "heat and light" within the Disk—is not confined to the Disk itself, but is present and active, and beneficent (life-giving) wherever the rays of the Sun reach. The symbol is found "in every sculpture," a fact that marks the stress that the king put upon it. And it is "an utterly new type in Egypt, distinct from all previous sculptures" (Petrie 1904: 214).

Here, and more so perhaps in the hymns, we find the assertion that the Sun-rays are the Sun's energy, everywhere present, everywhere active. It is through them that He manifests Himself—a truth that modern science has recognized and of which modern therapy is trying more and more to make a practical use. And it is in considering the Sun-rays, agents both of heat and light, that Akhenaten grasped intuitively the great scientific truth which gives the whole structure of his teaching a solid foundation of intellectual certitude so rarely found in more popular religions. He realized the equivalence of heat and light and of all forms of energy. Rightly has Petrie written:

> No one—Sun-worshipper or philosopher—seems to have realized until within this century, the truth which was the basis of Akhenaten's worship, that the rays of the Sun are the means of the Sun's action, the source of all life, power and force in the universe. The abstraction of regarding the radiant energy as all-important was quite disregarded until recent views of the conservation of force, of heat as a mode of motion, and the identity of heat, light and electricity have made us familiar with the scientific conception which was the characteristic feature of Akhenaten's new worship. (1904: 214)

Another assertion within the hymns which tallies amazingly with the modern conception of the ultimate reality, is the one previously noted: "Thou Thyself art alone, but there are millions of powers of life in Thee, to make Thy creatures live." It is the assertion that:

(1.) There is finally no other reality but the One. (Thou art alone.)

(2.) The One contains within It infinite possibilities of life and the tendency to bring them forth into actual existence. That is the only meaning we can ascribe to the words "millions of powers of life" or "millions of vitalities in Thee."

(3.) Consequently, "creation" is not the miraculous act through which an agent, distinct by nature from the created things, causes them to spring out of nothingness, but the gradual manifestation into actual existence of the different possibilities, latent within the One. In other words, that the One supreme reality is immanent in all things, and that it has been and is forever producing all the endless variety of the universe out of Itself.

If we regard that one object of worship—that essence of the Sun, which is the essence of the solar system—as the same mysterious entity that modern science calls 'energy' and places at the root of all existence, material or imma-terial, then what I have said of it and of the meaning of creation becomes clear. That idea of the infinity of beings as transient products of one fundamental agent, power, and substance, essence of life as well as of so-called inanimate existence. That conception of a world in which, strictly speaking, there is no place for pure passivity, but where the inanimate is just life at the lowest stage, is indeed the one suggested by the boldest generalization of our times.

We may call it metaphysical, in a way. But it is no airy metaphysics; no outcome of pure fancy; no dialectical invention. It fits in with the accumulated experience of men who have learnt to measure the infinitely small and the infi-nitely great, and to see the universe at different scales of vision. It should per-haps as yet be called a hypothesis rather than a fact. But it is the hypothesis that explains the facts which we know: it is the philosophical projection of the science of our times. And one can only marvel at the intuition of the adoles-cent king who grasped it 3,300 years ago.

THE DIVINE SPARK

It is a well-known fact that all kings of Egypt were looked upon first as "sons of Re" and later on as "sons of Amun." And this was no metaphor in the minds of the Egyptians, nor perhaps in the minds of the kings themselves. It was really believed that the god used to visit each queen destined to be a Pharaoh's mother in the form of her human husband, and become, by her, the actual physical father of the future king. On many Pharaohs' monuments is pictured the story of this divine conception.

But Akhenaten never put forth any similar claim. He did, it is true, repeat-edly declare himself "Son of the living Aten"; but not in the miraculous sense his fathers had claimed to be "sons of Amun." No bas-relief, no painting, no evidence of any sort is to be found which could allow us to suppose that he regarded himself to be, physically, the son of aught but his earthly father, Amenhotep III. The idea of a miraculous conception is, in fact, incompatible with that of an impersonal God. And Akhenaten was too much of a rationalist not to avoid that contradiction. "Son of the living Aten," *i.e.*, "Son of God," he certainly did proclaim himself to be. But that was in an entirely different sense. His own divinity was, to him, a consequence of his unity with the one divine power-substance at the back of all existence—an implication of his experience of a state of super-normal consciousness in which he felt his subtle self identical, in nature, with the universal energy which he adored. In other words, we should see in this claim to divinity the expression of the innermost certitude of a self-realized soul who can say of the one ultimate reality: "I am That," of God: "I am He"; not merely the customary boast of a king of Egypt about his solar descent.

But the modern critical mind will ask: Why, then, that exclusive claim to the knowledge of the divine? Why the strange sentence: "There is none who knoweth Thee excepting Thy Son, Nefer-kheperu-Re Ua-en-Re" (Beautiful essence of the Sun, Only One of the Sun)? If the God whom Akhenaten worshipped was radiant energy, the principle of all life, present even in apparently inanimate matter, then how could he claim for himself the monopoly of wisdom? A personal God, still endowed with mysterious human feelings, could prefer one man to all others and reveal "His plans and His powers" to him alone. But surely an immanent God of the type of "the heat and light within the Disk" could not be accused of such partiality.

To understand the king's statement, we must not forget that he had in mind the *knowledge* concerning the ultimate one, not the presence of it. From the reality of cosmic energy at the root of all things, it would be rash to infer that the knowledge, *i.e.*, the clear consciousness of it, is universal. That clear consciousness of the essence of existence within the individual seems, in fact, excluded not only from apparently inanimate matter but also from the plants and from the lower and even higher animals, including nearly all men. *Every atom of matter contains the divine spark.* Every living creature is possessed with some dim awareness of it. Many men think themselves more fully conscious of its presence than they really are. Extremely few are able to realize that their essential identity with the ultimate principle of all things is not a myth, and that, in truth, "they are That." To those alone belong the knowledge of God and the wisdom "to understand His plans and His power." Akhenaten was undoubtedly one of them, and he was conscious of his knowledge.

We can infer, with a fair amount of safety, that among the crowd of courtiers who professed to have welcomed his rational religion, Akhenaten realized more and more that he was all alone. He could not help remarking the gap which existed already during his lifetime between the life of his followers and the pure doctrine of reason, love and truth, which he preached to them. And that, no doubt, convinced him that they entirely lacked the foundation of genuine religion which he possessed: the experience of an overwhelming truth which lay in them, but transcended them. No one indeed could understand "the plans and power" of his God unless one had that experience; unless one was, like himself, aware of the oneness of his individual essence with that of the Sun and of the whole universe.

In the passage quoted above, the king does not use the name under which he is now immortal, Akhenaten, but that under which he was generally known in his days: his prenomen, Nefer-kheperu-Re,[1] which means "Beautiful essence of the Sun." This may be a mere coincidence. It may also be a deliberate symbolical choice. "There is none who knoweth Thee excepting Thy Son, Nefer-kheperu-Re," may well mean that one could not penetrate the nature of the object of the king's worship, the solar and at the same time cosmic energy unless one was conscious of being, one's self, "the beautiful essence of the Sun," as Akhenaten was. Experience had taught him that it was not possible to transmit that consciousness; that, however much he would preach the existence of the one power-substance—of the Sun-disk, identical with the energy within the Disk—it would remain a meaningless mystery to all men save those who had realized their own innermost identity with that one thing.

He knew no man who, by his life, gave signs of possessing such enlightenment. He only knew for sure that he possessed it. And his strange words, which we have just recalled, can therefore be taken to mean, equally: "No one knows Thee save I, the only one who can call myself Thy Son," and: "No one knows Thee save that man who, as I am, is aware of his identity with Thee within his individual limitations, and who thus can be called Thy Son." The two interpretations are correct. The second is a consequence of Akhenaten's conception of immanent divinity, felt by him in the Sun and in himself; and also the recognition of the impossibility to transmit the knowledge of that ultimate reality: cosmic energy. The first is the recognition of his own unique position in the history of the world which he knew. In his days, within his surroundings, and even among the older religious teachers whose fame had come down to him, he could see no one conscious of the great truth which he had realized. He was, therefore, "the Only One of the Sun." And he admitted it without false modesty.

But his very conception of Godhead logically excluded any miraculous personal revelation. And it is reasonable to admit that, had he met any man having the same awareness as he of his ultimate oneness with the principle of all things, he would not have hesitated to salute in him a true "son of the Sun" or "son of God"—one of his rare equals.

---

[1] A Pharaoh had several names: his "Horus name," his "Nebty name," his "Golden Horus name," his "Prenomen," his "Son of Re name." The name by which a Pharaoh is generally known to history is his "Son of Re" name.

(1) A Rational Monism

We have seen how Akhenaten's teaching, as known through the hymns, is based upon an inner experience of universal unity and upon an intuition of genius, the correctness of which has been proved nowadays by our men of science. The first gives the Religion of the Disk that sort of certitude that lies in the concordance of reliable testimonies. The second gives it the intellectual certitude that forces us to accept a scientific hypothesis, when it explains facts. This can be said to sum up the positive value of the teaching from a rational point of view.

But the teaching is perhaps as remarkable for what is absent from it as for what it contains. As I have already tried to point out in the introductory chapter of this book, Akhenaten seems to have deliberately avoided the three things of which we find one or two at least linked up, throughout history, with every successful religion: a background of supernatural stories—*i.e.*, a mythology; miracles; and a theory concerning the destiny of the dead.

If we turn to the hymns which Akhenaten has left us, we can see in them practically nothing which could not be grasped in the fourteenth century BC by a Syrian, by an Indian as well as by an Egyptian; nothing which is not today able to appeal to any man, without his needing any preparation other than a heart open to beauty. The only thing that would require explanation is, in the shorter hymn, a reference to "the House of the Benben Obelisk…in the City of Akhet-aten, the Seat of Truth." We know that the Benben Obelisk was the immemorial symbol of the Sun, worshipped in Heliopolis, the "City of the pillar." According to the ancient tradition reflected in the Pyramid Texts, "the Spirit of the Sun visited the temple of the Sun from time to time, in the form of a Bennu bird, and alighted on the Ben-stone in the House of the Bennu in Anu." In recalling the Benben stone, Akhenaten, it would seem, wished to stress how deep were the roots of his exclusive cult of the Sun in the most revered tradition of Egypt. The worship of Aten was evolved out of that of the god of Heliopolis. And the "House of the Benben Obelisk" meant simply the main temple of the Sun in the king's new capital, also a sacred city. But apart from that allusion there is, in the two hymns and in the prayer composed by Akhenaten and inscribed upon his coffin, and in the references to his teaching in the courtier's tombs, not a word which needs any special knowledge of Egypt and of her beliefs, in order to be understood.

The very name of the Sun which comes back over and over again in every text of the time, whether composed by the king or by his followers, is neither Re, nor Khepera, nor Tem, nor even 'Horus of the Two Horizons,' but Aten, *i.e.*, the Disk, a noun designating the geometrical shape of the visible Sun—and which can be literally translated into any language.

The symbol of God was neither a human figure nor an animal with a particular history at the back of it, nor a disk encircled by a serpent, but simply the solar-disk with downward rays ending in hands, bestowing life to the earth. According to Budge, this symbol "never became popular in the country"; it was perhaps, like the rest of the Religion of the Disk, "too philosophical" for the Egyptians as for many other nations. But it was a truly rational symbol, free from any mythological connections and clear to any intelligent person.

The text of the hymns refers to no legends, to no stories, to no particular theogony. Instead, only to the beauty and beneficence of our parent star, to its light "of several colors," to its universal worship by men, beasts and the vegetable world; to the marvel of birth; to the joy of life; to the rhythm of day and night and of the seasons, determined by the Sun; and to the great idea that the heat and light within the solar-disk, the "Ka" or soul of the Disk, and the Disk itself, are one. We find here nothing but conceptions that need only common sense and sensitiveness to beauty. And in order to be understood in their full, not a theological but a rational—and also spiritual—preparation; not the knowledge of any mythology or even of any human history, but a scientific knowledge of the universe, coupled with a spirit of synthesis.

I can only here, once more, quote Sir Flinders Petrie, to whom the world owes so much in the whole field of Egyptology:

> In this hymn, all trace of polytheism and of anthropomorphism or theriomorphism has entirely disappeared. The power of the Sun to cause and regulate all existence is the great subject of praise; and careful reflection is shown in enumerating the mysteries of the power of the Aten exemplified in the animation of nature, reproduction, the variety of races, and the source of the Nile and watering by rain. It would tax anyone in our days to recount better than this the power and action of the rays of the Sun. And no conception that can be compared with this for scientific accuracy was reached for at least three thousand years after it. (1904: 218)

(2) ORDINARY MIRACLES

Another remarkable trait of the Religion of the Disk is that it seems to have been completely devoid of that belief in miracles which holds such a place in most of the more popular religions, both ancient and modern; a belief, nay, without which the fundamental dogmas of most great world-wide religions of today could not be accepted by their followers.

When we speak of "miracles" we mean any events, impossible according to the laws of nature, but of which one yet admits the occurrence, taking it to be the result of a special intervention of God in the natural scheme of things. It must be noted that any conception of immanent God excludes the idea of supernatural intervention on the part of God. And any rational view of the world, whether pantheistic, theistic or atheistic, excludes miracles altogether. It is therefore natural that Akhenaten never ascribed to the impersonal energy behind the Disk the occasional tendency, or even the capacity, to break the immovable laws of nature.

In reading the hymns, one has the impression that, to him, the order of nature and the mystery of life were quite marvelous enough in themselves, without man's needing to seek an occasion to praise the power and wisdom of the creator. We have already seen that he never attributed to himself a miraculous birth as other Pharaohs were accustomed to do. He could not see in what way even such an event as that could be more divine than the everyday mystery of a germ, nursed by the universal Life-force within the egg or within the womb, and becoming in course of time a young bird or a child.

Whether the king possessed or not the power of performing unusual deeds, in the manner of many religious teachers of all times, we do not know. In the praise of him by some of the most enthusiastic of his followers, there is not the slightest hint that he did. It is, of course, not impossible that he did. If one is to believe a tradition persisting for centuries after the downfall of Egypt, the technique of developing one's psychic powers beyond the ordinary credible limits was not uncommon among the priests of the Nile Valley. In it even lay, one may imagine, their unshakable hold over the minds of the people. And there would be nothing unnatural in supposing that a man who exercised in the new cult the functions of High-priest of the Sun, was able to take interest in such an art. Moreover, we know definitely that Akhenaten had assumed the age-old title borne by the High-priest of the Sun in Heliopolis: Urma—the seer, or "the great one of visions"—which, if taken in the literal sense, does imply some powers beyond the ordinary.

But in the light of the evidence now available, we should admit that, even if he did possess the capacity of working feats of wonder, he made no use of it. He preferred positive knowledge and the logical and beautiful expression of knowledge in his life and teaching, to the easy task of impressing ignorant crowds. It is also quite plausible that he never endeavored to cultivate the art of acquiring supra-normal command over the physical world, considering it as not essentially connected with spiritual development, and therefore as superfluous.

And not only does the founder of the Religion of the Disk claim no miraculous powers for himself, but there is, in the fragments concerning his creed which have come down to us, not an allusion whatsoever to occurrences defying the laws of nature. The very idea of such seems to have been alien to the spirit of the king's teaching.

(3) LIFE, NOT DEATH

Finally, Akhenaten appears to have given his followers no definite doctrine about death and the fate of the dead.[2] The custom of mummifying dead bodies, prevalent in Egypt from time immemorial, was observed under him and in his own case. He therefore surely did not discourage it. But it is doubtful whether he subscribed to the essential ideas about the hereafter that the Egyptians associated with it. It is doubtful also whether the personal views he may have had about the mystery of death were ever preached by him as a part of his teaching. For though the evidence on which all discussion of this subject is necessarily based is very scanty, there seem to be reasons for one to distinguish between his idea of the survival of the soul and that of his followers.

The only document which may be taken to express his own views is the prayer inscribed at the foot of his coffin, and probably composed by himself:

> I breathe the sweet breath which comes forth from Thy mouth; I behold Thy beauty every day. It is my desire that I may hear Thy sweet voice, even in the North wind, that my limbs may be rejuvenated with life through love of Thee. Give me Thy hands holding Thy spirit, that I may receive it and live by it. Call Thou upon my name unto eternity, and it shall never fail. (in Weigall 1922: 259)

It seems, from this prayer addressed to the one God, that Akhenaten believed in the survival of the individual soul after death. The "I" who speaks here is a personal consciousness. But it is difficult to imagine personal consciousness beyond death without some sort of survival of the body. We all feel that we owe much of what we are to the characteristic constitution of our various organs. If nothing is to remain of our material self under any form, then the only sort of immortality we can expect, if any at all, is the impersonal immortality of that which is, in us, common to all beings; substantial everlastingness, rather than individual immortality. Akhenaten seems to have been aware of this, and not to have separated the survival of the individual from some sort of hazy corporeality. At least, that is what I would imagine to be implied in words such as: "that my limbs may be rejuvenated with life through love of Thee."

No one can say whether those very same words also imply that the founder of the Religion of the Disk shared the age-old Egyptian belief in the

---

[2] "The Aten religion contained none of the beautiful ideas on the future life, with which we are familiar from the hymns and other compositions in the Book of the Dead" (Budge 1912: 121-122).

resurrection of the dead. It may be he did. It may be he did not. It may be that, in his eyes, the "limbs" that constitute, in eternity, the agent of individualization, were those not of the resurrected mummy but of some surviving "body" more subtle than the visible one. In Akhenaten's conception, there is no clear-cut line of demarcation between the material and the immaterial—between the everlasting "Ka" of the Sun-disk and the Disk itself, and doubtless also between the immortal "ka" of a man and that man's body.

There is no mention of the rising of the dead anywhere in the solitary prayer, just quoted, which reveals to us practically all we know of Akhenaten's own beliefs, or hopeful conjectures, on the subject of death. But one or two courtiers do express, in the inscriptions in their tombs, the wish that their "flesh might live upon the bones," which seems to imply the hope of resurrection. One of the most constant desires of nearly all the king's followers was to continue to see the Sun after death—"to go out to see the Sun's rays"; "to obtain a sight of the beauty of every recurring sunrise," etc… Many also prayed for more tangible happiness; for the unchanged favor of their royal Master in the world beyond the grave; for name and fame in this world of the living; even for a share of the consecrated food offered at the altar of the Sun, "a reception of that which has been offered in the temple"; "a drink offering in the temple of Aten."

Weigall, in his admiration for the inspired young king, has endeavored to present him as the most outstanding precursor of Christianity in the Pagan world. And he attributes to him, precisely for that reason, ideas of the hereafter little different from those of an honest church-going Englishman—except, of course, for the important fact that "we hear nothing of hell" (1922: 121) in his teaching. Those ideas are much too precise, even in their necessary vagueness, to tally with the very vague references in the prayer I have mentioned, and somewhat too Christian-like to be ascribed to the world's first rationalist. Moreover, it is noteworthy that Weigall quotes only extracts from the inscriptions in the courtiers' tombs, and never the prayer which he himself holds to be "composed by Akhenaten" (ibid.: 248). And there is a difference in tone and in spirit between that prayer and those inscriptions.

From the prayer, nothing precise about Akhenaten's view of death can be pointed out, save perhaps that he believed in the survival of the individual under some much subtler state of corporeality. Also, he considered the universal energy within the Sun to be the principle of the new life, no less than of life under the form we know it. This seems to be the sense of "Give me Thy hands, holding Thy spirit, that I may receive it and live by it." The words: "that my limbs may be rejuvenated with life through love of Thee," may also imply that other idea that love of the supreme reality is the condition of consciousness, in that life beyond death which Akhenaten expected for himself.

Apart from these conjectures, which the text of the prayer suggests, we know nothing of his personal conception of the hereafter.

From this negative evidence it can be gathered that Akhenaten definitely rejected all that appeared to him as irrational in the Egyptian traditions regarding death. He surely did away with all the magic intertwined with them, and he may have had sufficient doubts to "disbelieve" in the Last Judgment and in the dogma of reward and punishment once and forever. If his courtiers omitted so much of the conventional funerary symbolism in their tombs, it is because he saw in it something meaningless, perhaps even harmful, and forbade it. But the positive instance of his followers' beliefs in immortality does not necessarily indicate, in a parallel manner, what were his personal views. Nothing proves that he subscribed to all the hopes which they express in their inscriptions.

From all this one may infer that, whatever were his personal conjectures concerning the hereafter, Akhenaten did not make them an article of his teaching, but allowed his disciples to solve the problem of death as they liked, provided the solutions they would choose were not too flagrantly childish. The mythology of the netherworld, as the Egyptians had believed in it for centuries was, to him, a network of "ridiculous fictions." And as Budge (1923: 95) adds, he actually gave his followers "nothing to put in the place of these fictions," because there was, indeed, nothing to give them. And as a rationalist that he was, he seems to have been much less definite about all he said regarding the possibilities of the next world, than he had been in his assertions about the realities of this.

He appears simply never to have pronounced himself on the problem of the hereafter. Perhaps this was because he deemed that problems of this world and this life should be solved first, perhaps also because he felt less sure of the solidity of his own conjectures about death than of that of his positive intuition of the ultimate essence: heat-and-light within the Sun, and world-consciousness within himself. He cancelled all that which struck him as definitely meaningless or absurd. He tolerated only such remnants of the past as were but harmless customs—for instance, the habit of embalming the dead—or age-old beliefs which were as difficult to disprove as to justify and which, therefore, might have contained some spark of truth.

In his teaching, he seems neither to have asserted nor denied the current Egyptian dogma of the resurrection of the flesh. It may be that he associated it with the idea of individual survival which would imply, it seems, corporeality. But what corporeality after death meant to him, is not clear to us. The one thing which can be said is that his uncertain attitude towards the problem of death is perfectly consistent with that rigorous rationalism that I remarked all through his doctrine, along with the inspiration that fills it. They are the signs of a truly scientific spirit.

Of Reality and Truth

It seems right to believe, with Budge, that the fact that he put "nothing in the place" of the old fictions about the next world had the result of turning the Egyptians away from Akhenaten and his teaching. Not, as Budge says, because "being of African origin, they never understood or cared for philosophical abstractions," but because they were foolish, and craved for illusions in the absence of available knowledge.

We may add that the omission of any "mythology" and of miracle-stories from the teaching had the same immediate effect. People always wished to be entertained, moved, and astonished by marvelous tales, and made to believe them. And all the great successful religions, when based originally on purely philosophical principles—as Buddhism—have seen more and more miraculous narratives creep into their sacred literature as years passed on, and as they spread to further countries. Had the Religion of the Disk not been nipped in the bud, it is probable that the same thing would have happened with it, in course of time.

But if the absence of what makes a religion popular condemned it, from the start, never to spread of its own impetus; if its founder himself, doubtless feeling how far too rational his teaching was for the needs of the mob, never tried to preach it, this was not without an advantage. Popular religions of Akhenaten's time, that long held sway over nations, have died out. And they could not possibly be revived, now or in the future, precisely because of the mythology and supernatural stories and particular views about death and funerary rites which overload them and hide the amount of truth that they did contain, and make them the products of particular civilizations.

And nearer to us, in our own world, the greatest obstacle to the proselytism of the well-known international religions still alive, is that they too are irremediably linked up with a particular background of history and legend, stamped with a definite *couleur locale*. Also, they appear inseparable from such supernatural events as the modern mind is no longer ready to accept. Islam cannot be preached to England or Germany detached from the marvelous stories that once stirred the admiration of the medieval Arab tent-dweller. Christianity cannot be preached to India and China detached from its Jewish and Greco-Roman associations. And in Europe itself Renan was already conscious that, if anything would one day make people skeptical and indifferent towards it, it would be those very miracles that once made its fortune.

But Akhenaten's teaching, devoid of the three things that have assured the success of other doctrines, is also free from the germs of decay contained in them. Logically, it can be revived, now and in any age to come, in any place where rational thinking is more than an empty profession. The absence of miracles, as well as of any positive answer to the insoluble question of death, makes it a religion that the critical mind can prefer to many others. Its rationality, one of the most potent causes of its failure in Egypt, in the days of its founder, could therefore one day become the main source of its appeal to the disinterested, truth-seeking intelligentsia of all the world. This hope, however premature it might still seem, is not unjustified, considering the nature of the teaching and the history of man's religious evolution.

Fig. 7: Nefertiti makes an offering to the Aten.

CHAPTER 6

THE WAY OF LOVE

We have seen how Akhenaten's two hymns to the Sun which have come down to us suggest an idea of the divine which, as Petrie has so effectively pointed out, tallies with "our modern scientific conceptions." But that is not all. The impersonal God whom the young king worshipped is no less inspiring to the heart of the mystic in search of absolute love, than to the clear intellect of the rationalist in search of logical and experimental accuracy. He is the "Lord of Love" no less than the Lord of Truth.

As Weigall (1922: 105) says, quoting the Christian Scriptures, never in history "had a man conceived a god who 'so loved the world.'" But there is, between the love of Aten for the world and the love of the personal God of the Gospel, all the difference that separates a link of impersonal necessity from one of human attachment.

We must not forget the nature of Aten, who is neither a god in the image of man, nor even an individual power of any description, but the ultimate impersonal reality behind all existence. The love of such a God for the millions and millions of lives which He brought forth from Himself is something different from the love of an individual parent for his offspring. True, Akhenaten calls his God the "Father-and-Mother of all which He hath made." But if our interpretation of Aten be the right one, then that double appellation, far from containing any anthropomorphic idea, most probably symbolizes the two complementary aspects of the one ultimate essence: *the active*, forever urging new forms and new lives out of dim latent possibilities, and *the passive*, the sensitive receptacle of all those possibilities, matrix of actual existence. In other words, both the one everlasting power of *differentiation*, and the everlasting and ever-differentiated *oneness*. The individual parent and the offspring, however closely linked, are separate bodies with a separate consciousness. The "Father-and-Mother" of the universe and the universe itself are not. The latter is the visible and diversified expression of the former invisible and indivisible one—the energy within the Disk and within the universe. Matter is but an aspect of it.

The love of Aten for the world is the stable unifying power that underlies all that is diverse and transient—all that is created. "Thou bindest them with Thy love" means: "Through their common relation to Thee, the one essence of all things, they are one in their diversity—'bound to Thee,' and bound together within their apparent separateness." In Breasted's version of the longer hymn we read: "Thou art Re; Thou hast carried them all away captive; Thou bindest them by Thy love…" The word "captive" would seem to indicate a link of complete dependence of the creatures upon the creator. They are bound to Him as to the final condition of their existence.

In that link rests the secret of their link to one another. They are one in Him, because first of all they are one with Him, as children are one with a loving parent, and much more so.

ATEN, BRINGER OF LIFE

But apart from this relation of fact between the ultimate energy and all that exists, the hymns clearly point out to a relation of intention. In Aten's love "for all He hath made," there is something more than the bond of physical and logical unity which we have tried to analyze. There is not, of course, that personal love, which only a god in the image of man can feel for each of his creatures; but there is some immanent finality which operates, in each individual case, as if it were the sign of God's special individual care; a tendency to well-being which nature encourages and helps; an untiring goodness, which strikes one at every step as underlying the whole scheme of things.

That seems to be the truth expressed in Akhenaten's beautiful passages about the kindness of Aten to the child and to the young bird, mere instances of His solicitude for all creatures. The marvel of pre-natal existence—the patient evolution of a cell into a full-grown individual—is recalled, with all the finality inherent to it, in a few words:

> Thou art a nurse in the womb, giving breath to vivify that which Thou hast made… Thou giveth breath to him (the young bird) inside the egg, to make him live. Thou makest for him his mature form so that he can crack the shell (being) inside the egg…

God does His best. He "gives breath" to every young living thing; He equips it with organs marvelously adjusted; He helps it to grow, before its birth, and feeds it afterwards, for some time at least, that it may have a chance to fulfill its purpose which is to live, to enjoy the sunshine and to be beautiful, in the full-bloom of health and happiness. And though it is not said in the hymns, one feels, from the very tone of the king's words, the moral truth that they imply. One feels that, in his eyes, it is man's duty to collaborate with the universal Parent, the life-giving Sun; to love all creatures and to help them to live; not merely to do no harm to them, but to see to their welfare, to the utmost of his capacity. Life, which is such a masterpiece of divine love, is not to be considered lightly. And the welfare of anything that lives, especially of any creature that is helpless, is to be the object of our personal care. God Himself has pointed out the way to us by the example of His untiring solicitude.

It is remarkable that Akhenaten seems to give no less importance to the young bird—standing for the whole animal world—than to the human baby. The admiration he expresses for the loving care of Him who brings the embryo to maturity and "provideth its needs" is equal in both cases. And one has the impression that the "Heat-and-Light-within-the-Disk"—his God—knows nothing of the childish partiality of the man-made gods in favor of the human species. Those gods, conceived centuries after the inspired Pharaoh, appear indeed as glorified deities—which, no doubt, some of them originally were—raised by the pride of their worshippers to the leadership of a mere extended tribe, mankind.

In the hymn from which we have quoted the above passage, there is another reference in which different countries are enumerated: "Thou didst create the world according to Thy desire, Syria, and Nubia and the land of Egypt..." Commenting on the fact that the two tributary nations are named before Egypt, Weigall, following the pious trend of thought that characterizes his whole book, says:

> Akhenaten believed that his God was the Father of all mankind and that the Syrian and the Nubian were as much under His protection as the Egyptian. The religion of the Aten was to be a world religion. This is a greater advance in ethics than may be at first apparent; for the Aten thus becomes the first deity who was not tribal or not national ever conceived by mortal mind. This is the Christian's understanding of God, though not the Hebrew conception of Jehovah. This is the spirit which sends the missionary to the uttermost parts of the earth; and it was such an attitude of mind which now led Akhenaten to build a temple to the Aten in Palestine, possibly at Jerusalem itself, and another far up in the Sudan. (1922: 166)

Before ascribing a definite date to the religious books of the East, it is difficult to say whether Aten was or not the first universal God "ever conceived by mortal mind." But if, by his belief in a God who was the Father of the foreigners as well as of the Egyptians, Akhenaten was in advance of the old Hebrew idea of Jehovah, then surely his conception of Aten puts him no less in advance of Christianity itself—nay, in advance of *any* creed which makes man, and not life, the centre of its theory of creation and the basis of its scale of values. It is precisely this entire absence, not merely of nationalism and of imperialism, but also of any form of anthropomorphism which raises the young Pharaoh far above so many later religious teachers and sets him, decidedly, ahead of our present times.

GOD SO LOVES THE WORLD

The impersonal energy which radiates as heat and light in the life-giving Disk of the Sun—Aten—loves the world and all that lives upon it. In other words, *Nature is indiscriminately, impartially kind.* The tragedies that we witness every day are man's doing. God has given, to every young individual, health and the desire to enjoy the daylight. He intended it to live its span of years, not to die miserably. Even out of destruction and death He makes life spring out again, causing tender green shoots to appear on the branches of the mutilated trees, and new trees to grow out of the roots of those that were felled. To Him, life is an end in itself. And at every new attempt He makes to bring forth a living thing, again at its birth He lavishes upon it His gifts of health and beauty, possibilities of development into the perfection of its species, promises of happiness.

Such was the essential of Akhenaten's teaching concerning the love of God. He seems, at least from the little we now possess of his religious poems, to have ignored evil entirely. And perhaps he actually did so, for not only in the hymns, but also in the numerous inscriptions which cover the walls of his followers' tombs, "the destructive qualities of the Sun were never referred to," not to speak of all the crimes against life that are allowed to be committed under His face all over the earth. That omission, as I have already said in a former chapter, cannot be explained by supposing the king to have been blind to the existence of suffering as a fact. That would be absurd. True, the surroundings he had created for himself were exceedingly beautiful. But he knew that the wide world extended far beyond them, and beyond his own beneficent influence.

Moreover, there never was a town on earth where people were totally free from anger and greed, cruelty and cowardice, the sources of the evil actions that produce suffering. And Akhet-aten, though the "seat of Truth," was surely no exception, for men dwelt there. And the young Prophet of sunshine and joy must have known how limited was his control over other people's bad instincts, even at a few yards from his peaceful palace. Yet, he sang the love of God, in spite of it all. He deeply felt that there was, at the birth of every new life, equipped for happiness, the triumph of an inexhaustible Power of love, which governs the universe. The newly-born creature might not be left to enjoy the full-bloom of life for which its body and soul were made. The possibility of enjoying it was, nevertheless, the result of the whole finality of its pre-natal development, the outcome of a divine solicitude. Health and happiness were its birthright, according to the decrees of the immense immanent Love that sustains all creation, the Soul of the universe—God.

Seen in the light of the young king's super-conscious insight into the mystery of existence, the effects of human wickedness appeared perhaps as but surface ripples, hardly perturbing the calm abyss of eternal Life and infinite Love. That is possible. However it be, he did not ask the reason why such ripples exist, because he knew there was no answer to the question. It would seem that he brushed aside the problem of evil deliberately, as something which the human mind, however exalted, cannot solve. And instead of seeking in vain an explanation where there was none, he absorbed himself in the contemplation of the one unpolluted Source of health, life and love: the energy within the Sun.

UNIVERSAL LOVE

No less than the love of God for the world, manifested in the untiring beneficence of our parent star, Akhenaten has stressed the love of all living creatures for their common Father, whose heat and light has brought them forth and sustains them, generation after generation.

All men love Him and bow down to Him, whatever be their other professed gods. "They live when Thou shinest upon them..." says the inspired author of the hymns; "their eyes, when Thou risest, turn their gaze upon Thee..." "Every heart beateth high at the sight of Thee, for Thou risest as their Lord." And also: "All men's hands are stretched out in praise of Thy rising"... "O Lord of every land, Thou shinest upon them; O Aten of the day, great in majesty," or, in the translation of Griffith, reproduced by Petrie: "Thou art throughout their Lord, even in their weakness, O Lord of the land that risest for them, Aten of the day, revered in every distant country."

In fact, every nation in the neighborhood of Egypt paid homage to the Sun under a different name. And however narrow might have been their conception of the God of Light, and however debased might have been their forms of worship, still it was to Him that went their praise. They loved Him and revered Him without knowing Him.

And distant peoples and tribes of which the king of Egypt could not possibly have heard, also rendered divine honors to the same fiery Disk at His dawning and setting. It was a fact that, while Akhenaten's poems were sung to His glory "in the hall of the House of the Benben Obelisk and in every temple in Akhet-aten, the seat of truth," the Aryan clans, slowly pouring into India, were exalting Him in the hymns of the Rig-Veda. Wild tribes from the north of Europe and Asia sang the beauty of His hazy smile over endless snow-bound plains and dark forests. And at the eastern end of the earth, the primitive people of Japan doubtless already hailed His rising out of the Pacific Ocean. And still farther to the east and to the south, men of undiscovered isles and continents praised Him, in speeches now long forgotten, with strange rites of which we shall never know.

And thus it was true that the whole world was full of His name. From the Nile to the Andes, and from the frozen beaches over which He sheds His midnight rays to the luxuriant isles that smile in His golden light, in the midst of phosphorescent seas, it was true that "all men's hands" were "stretched out in praise of His rising." Akhenaten probably did not know how big our planet is; nor had he any idea of the farthermost lands of dawn and sunset bordering the two great oceans. Yet, with a sure insight of truth, he proclaimed his God: "Thou Aten of the day, revered in every distant land."

He was aware of the universality of Sun-worship, that oldest and most natural religion in the world, of which still today one could find concrete traces in the rites and customs and festivals of more intricate, more anthropomorphic cults. He was aware also that, if any religion could one day claim to conquer the earth and unite all enlightened mankind, it could be none but this one. The worldwide concert of man's praise to the Sun, of which the dim echo resounded in his heart, clumsy, childish, discordant as it was, filled him with joy and glorious hopes. It was the first expression of the whole human race groping in quest of the real God. Its final expression could be but the worship of the one essence of all existence, cosmic energy, manifested in the heat and light of our parent star; the rational cult of the Sun, which he had forestalled in Akhet-aten, his sacred City.

NATURE BASKS IN DIVINE LIGHT

There is more. Aten is not the God of man alone. We have seen that He loves all creatures impartially and treats them with equal solicitude. It is shown in the hymns no less clearly that all creatures love and worship Him, each in the manner of its species:

- "Every creature that Thou hast made skippeth towards Thee...";
- "All the beasts frisk about on their feet; all the feathered fowl rise up from their nests and flap their wings with joy, and circle around in praise of the Living Aten..."
- "Beasts and cattle of all kinds settle down upon the pastures..."
- "the feathered fowl fly about over their marshes, their feathers (*i.e.*, their wings) praising Thy 'Ka'..."
- "All the cattle rise up on their legs; creatures that fly and insects of all kinds spring into life when Thou risest up on them..."
- "The fishes in the river swim up to greet Thee."

And it is not only quadrupeds and birds, insects and fishes that take part in the general chorus of joy and praise that rises from the earth to the Sun; "shrubs and vegetables flourish" when Thou risest upon them; "buds burst into flower, and the plants which grow on the waste lands send up shoots at Thy rising; they drink themselves drunk before Thy face."

There are two ideas, quite different from each other, expressed in these few quotations from the hymns: on one hand that all creatures *rejoice* at the sight of the Sun; on the other that they all *worship* the Sun. The first is a matter of everyday observation that many a sensitive soul would probably have stressed in a poem to the glory of the life-giving Disk; a commonplace truth which indeed has been emphasized in various antique songs of unknown date and authorship, and which implies no special insight on the part of whoever grasps it; an obvious fact. The second idea implies the belief in the unity of all life and the brotherhood of creatures, and provides the basis of a whole religious and moral outlook.

Apart from Petrie, most authors among those who appreciate Akhenaten's teaching seem to do so on account of his God being the God of all nations, as opposed to the hosts of national and tribal deities worshipped all over the ancient world. But a closer reading of the hymns in a totally unprejudiced spirit would have revealed a feeling of truly universal brotherhood much more comprehensive than that expressed by any later religious teacher, west of India, with the noble exception of a few Greeks—such as Apollonius of Tyana. The fatherhood of the Sun implied, in Akhenaten's eyes, the brotherhood of all sentient beings, human and non-human. The point deserves to be stressed.

As I have remarked, there are two distinct ideas in the hymns, with regard to living creatures. The joy of life, and the excitement that the appearing of daylight produces in all beings, from man to plant, is one thing. The feeling it reveals, no doubt, in the author of the hymns, a heart open to universal understanding and to sympathy for all that lives. But that alone does not necessarily imply any religious doctrine about the unity of man and beast. In fact, saints full of the same tender love for dumb creatures have honored, in course of time, religions according to the teachings of which man remains the special object of God's solicitude and the measure of all values. Saint Francis of Assisi, for instance, called all creatures his "brothers." And long before him a follower of the Prophet of Islam, Abu Hurairah, so tradition says, preferred to cut off a piece of his mantle rather than disturb a cat that had gone to sleep upon it. Had Akhenaten only spoken of the thrill that the rising Sun sends through all flesh; had even touching stories come down to us concerning his kindness to animals, yet we would not be able to say, on those grounds alone, what was the exact place of animals in the Religion of the Disk. Such evidence would have borne witness to the king's value as a man. But it would have added little to our knowledge of his teaching.

Fortunately, he said more. Not only did he look upon the joyous demonstrations of the animal world at daybreak as marks of love for the Sun, but he also considered them as unmistakable expressions of adoration. Birds, said he, "flap their wings with joy, and circle round in praise of the living Aten." And that also is not all. One holding the general views inherited from the Bible by modern mankind would perhaps be inclined to concede that animals do pay some sort of homage to the material Sun-disk that shines above them, without looking up to any more subtle God, creator and animator of the Disk itself. But Akhenaten, following to the end the logical implications of an entirely different view of the universe, boldly asserts that the God whom beasts and birds worship is the self-same invisible, intangible essence of all being, manifested in the Sun, whom man reveres "in every distant country"—the "Ka," or soul of the Sun; *the Soul of the World*. "The feathered fowl fly about over their marshes, their wings adoring Thy 'Ka.'"

Not that the young Pharaoh probably believed animals to be aware of the nature of that all-pervading supreme reality to which we have referred in the preceding chapter. He did not hold all men, also, or even the majority of men, to be conscious of what they really worshipped in the visible Sun. The sentence we have already quoted: "Thou art in my heart, and there is none who knoweth Thee save Thy Son, Nefer-kheperu-Re Ua-en-Re..." (Beautiful-essence-of-the-Sun, Only-one-of-the-Sun) is sufficient to show what an aristocratic conception he had of what is, properly speaking, "religion."

But just as he believed that men all tend to the consciousness of the one essence and worship It in the Sun, in spite of their ignorance, so he held that beasts and birds, even insects and fishes—all living beings—dimly tend to the same ultimate knowledge. They already worship the same principle of universal life, cosmic energy, without being able to conceive its nature, or even to think of it. They are, like the majority of men, vaguely aware of something fundamental and supreme, which they feel in the heat and light of the Sun; in the magic touch of His life-giving beams. And they worship it, each one to the uttermost capacity of his individual nature and of his particular species. That seems to have been Akhenaten's view of the relation of animals to God. They were, in his eyes, religious beings of the same nature as man; capable of prayer and adoration, in a vaguer manner but perhaps with no less elementary emotional intensity. Otherwise the word "Ka" would have no sense in the above references.

ATEN, FATHER OF ALL LIFE

Of plants, it is not said in the hymns whether or not, in their thrill at the touch of Aten's golden beams, there enters any element of adoration. Yet, if the leap of the fish towards the surface of the water is considered as an act of "greeting" the rising Sun, it seems hardly possible not to see in the water-lilies that "drink themselves drunk" (of His radiance) "before His face," living creatures enjoying the maximum of ecstatic joy that their nature permits. The king's words, "they drink themselves drunk," seem to imply, in their case also, a sort of religious intoxication, a holy rapture, as the warm sun-rays enter the open flowers and reach down into their hearts.

In other words, far from setting up a definite line of demarcation between man and the living world outside man, and considering our species endowed with special rights by a god who made the rest of creatures for its use; far from forestalling, that is to say, the common view of later monotheistic creeds, from that of the Jews onwards, Akhenaten looked upon all sentient beings as children of the same father—the Sun. All are co-worshippers of the same ultimate God, cosmic energy, made visible and tangible in the Sun; as brothers, identical in nature, different only inasmuch as the consciousness of the supreme one is more or less developed in each individual. And just as all nations were united, in his eyes, by the fact that they all revere the "Father-and-Mother" of life in various tongues and with various inadequate rites, so were all living species united to one another and to man by the worship of the one Cosmic God.

For such was Aten, the God of all animals (and plants) as well as of all men; the God of all men, in fact, only because He was, primarily and essentially, the God of life in general. The value of the Religion of the Disk lies precisely in the fact that it is perhaps the only religion fit for cats and all beasts no less than for men, and supermen. Its bold views concerning the oneness of matter and energy may well be understood only by a few human beings, even today. But its visible object of worship—the Sun—is, and indeed ever will be, the only manifestation of God which beasts, and birds, and fishes, and plants, and all possible forms of life can be expected to appreciate in their own way, no less than we do in ours, and to worship, if they are to worship anything. However simple be a creed, it can only be extended to all mankind—not beyond. Nor can any seer, any prophet, any deified hero receive the allegiance of creatures other than men. Nor can even any idol be worshipped by dumb beasts. But the Sun appeals to all, inspires all, is loved and worshipped by all, from the philosophizing devotee of intangible energy down to the cat, the cock, the fish, the sunflower.

And the young founder of the Religion of the Disk himself would have, no doubt, seen in the movement of the beautiful sensitive feline stretching out its velvet paws with pleasure as it winks at the Sun, and in the raising of his own hands in praise of Him, two parallel gestures of worship—two expressions of the universal love of finite, individual life for the unknown, infinite and impersonal energy, source of all life.

THE PRINCE OF PEACE

The love of God for the whole world, and the love of the whole world for God, are thus clearly expressed in the shorter and in the longer hymns. The love of creatures for one another, especially of man for creatures, is not referred to. The hymns are poems in praise of the splendor, power, and goodness of God, nothing more. They contain but statements of fact. And the love of man for his brothers of different races and different species is not a fact, even today. But it is the natural feeling of whoever realizes, as Akhenaten did, that all creatures, from the superman down to the meanest particle of life in the depth of the ocean, have sprung into existence out of the same divine source—the Sun. All are sustained by the action of the same vivifying rays and that, each one in its own way, they all adore the only God, whose face is the resplendent Disk of our parent star. And in that respect, one can surely say that it is implied in the hymns—nay, that it is the very spirit of Akhenaten's teaching.

The example of the young Pharaoh's life reveals better than any song the practical implications of his religion. And there is sound evidence that, in various important circumstances, his action, or his restraint from action, was prompted by nothing else but that universal love, natural to a true worshipper of the Sun, which also pervaded his everyday life.

I have spoken of his love for his consort and children, nearly always represented at his side, in paintings and bas-reliefs, in the most unconventional attitudes. We have also mentioned his generosity towards his followers, on whom the contemporary artists portray him lavishing every possible mark of favor. But pleasant and instructive as they are, those scenes of idyllic married happiness and of friendly patronage should not be mistaken for instances of universal love. They no doubt show us, in Akhenaten, a delicate soul, sensitive to the innocent joys of family life and of friendship. They may add to the particular charm he possesses even apart from his teaching. They appeal to us especially because they make of him, in our eyes, a man like ourselves. They bestow upon him the attractiveness of living life. The eternal actuality of the feelings which they betray bridges the gaping gulf of time, and makes the founder of the long-forgotten Religion of the Disk young and lovely forever.

But there is, after all, nothing in them which deserves our moral admiration, save perhaps the perfect frankness with which the king allowed them to be rendered. Many men have loved but one woman and have lived with her a peaceful domestic life, without sharing anything of Akhenaten's greatness. And all teachers are inclined to be kind to those who seem to show a keen interest in their message. As for the young Pharaoh's affection for his little daughters, it is but natural. And if one infers, from the fondness he displays towards them, that he probably liked children in general, that is also a trait which many fathers would have in common with him.

Another instance of Akhenaten's impartial love for human beings is to be found in his attitude towards foreigners—nay, towards rebels, enemies of his country and of his power—and finally in his behavior towards his personal enemies.

What one could call the young king's "internationalism" and his "pacifism" are perhaps, of all the remarkable aspects of his mental outlook, the ones that appeal the most to many modern historians. And it does indeed stir our interest to find such traits as these developed, and that, to the extent we shall see, in a youth of the early 14th century BC.

It has been observed that Syria and Nubia (Ethiopia) are named before Egypt in the reference quoted above from the longer hymn. The detail is significant. But quite apart from it, the tone of the whole passage is in striking contrast with that of earlier Egyptian hymns addressed to the Sun-god considered as a local god, and especially with that of such poems as the famous Hymn of Victory composed by a priest of Amun under Thotmose III, both in honor of the great god of Thebes and of the conqueror of Syria, and characteristic of the spirit of imperial Egypt. And the history of the king's dealings with foreigners, both friends and foes, fully confirms the impression left by his words.

The presence among his dearest disciples of a man like Panehsi, an Ethiopian, shows that he was free from any racial prejudice in his estimation of individuals. He was, though, the very last man to ignore the natural, God-ordained separation of races, nay, although he considered it as an essential aspect of that diversity within order, which characterizes Aten's creation.[1] But more eloquent than all is the impartial view he seems to have taken of the rights of foreign countries.

The whole story of Akhenaten's dealings with his vassal states is amazing from beginning to end. It clashes with all one knows of the established relations between subject people of any race and at any epoch, and their natural overlord. It cannot be explained as the result either of incapacity or of negligence on the part of a king whose administration at home appears to have been firm, and whose sense of responsibility is out of question. It can only be regarded, as we shall stress later on, as one of those material tragedies that follow the application of the noblest principles to the conduct of the affairs of a barbaric world. It shows that Akhenaten was not the man able to keep what Thotmose I and Thotmose III had conquered.

---

[1] Thou settest every man in his place...
Their tongues are diverse in speech,
Their shape likewise, and the color of their skins;
for, as a Divider, Thou dividest the strange peoples.
(Longer Hymn).

But it shows, also, that the reason why he could not keep it is that he was hundreds of years in advance of his times—and of our times. For the principle which guided him, in his systematic refusal to help his loyal vassals in their struggle against the "nationalist" elements of Syria, seems to have been that of the right of the Syrians, as a people distinct from the Egyptians, to dispose of themselves and solve their own problems. He saw clearly that some of them were in favor of Egyptian domination; the majority, however, seemed to be against it. The best course for him was to let them fight out the question of their future status without interfering. The interest of Egypt, of his supporters, and of himself mattered little, if opposed to that idea of the right of all nations to live free under the same life-giving Sun, the father of all. And it is because he loved all men impartially in his universal God of life and love that Akhenaten believed in that right, as in something fundamental.

There is still more. While so many people, even today, try to defend the maintenance of a status quo resulting from old wars of aggression, it is, no doubt, staggering to think of a young man proclaiming the brotherhood of all nations and their right to freedom, 3,300 years ago. But one might argue that Akhenaten was, as his detractors call him, a "religious fanatic," and that such people have no feelings but for what touches their cherished doctrines. The final test of his love for all men lies in his attitude towards the bitterest enemies of his teaching, the priests of Amun.

We know that he closed the temples of their god; that he abolished his cult, and that the enormous revenues which his predecessors formerly lavished upon it he henceforth used for the glorification of the one God, for the embellishment of Akhet-aten, and for different works of public utility. We also know that he confiscated the scandalous wealth of the priests and did away with their influence. But, apart from that, he caused no harm to be done to them.

Sir Wallis Budge, who seems bent on finding fault with all that Akhenaten did, compares him with the Fatimide Khalif Al-Hakim, who reigned in Cairo 2,500 years later, and tells us that "it would be rash to assume that persons who incurred the king's displeasure in a serious degree were not removed by the methods that have been well known at Oriental courts from time immemorial" (1923: 107). But he himself admits, after recalling Al-Hakim's wholesale massacres of his enemies, that "we have no knowledge that such atrocities were committed in Akhet-aten," so that the fact of Akhenaten being an "Oriental" king seems to be the only basis on which the 20th century historian puts forth his damaging assumption—a very flimsy basis indeed.

Baikie has singled out Budge's comment as a characteristic example of what prejudice can bring a serious writer to say, once it has got the best of his good sense. I add that, had any act of violence taken place, at Akhenaten's command or with his consent, against the opponents of his rational creed, the scribes in the pay of the priests of Amun would surely not have failed to give us a graphic account of it, once the national gods had been restored under Tutankhamen. The absence of any such account suffices to lead one to believe that, beyond dispossessing them of their excessive riches, Akhenaten never harmed the men who hated him the most, though he had every power to do so. His behavior suggests that, in his eyes, the awareness of the universal fatherhood of the Sun implied a broad humanity; a sincere love extended, in practical life, to all men, including one's foes; including those who, in their ignorance, scorn the real God in favor of dead formulas and spurious symbols.

JOYOUS OFFERINGS

It implied more. As I have said, it implied love towards all creatures, our brothers, which the Sun has brought into life not for our use, but for each one of them to flourish in health and beauty, and to praise Him to the utmost capacity of its species. Even the plants are created for a higher purpose inherent in their nature. It is said in the longer hymn: "Thy beams nourish every field; Thou risest and they live; they germinate for Thee."

One would like to possess more positive evidence of Akhenaten's personal attitude towards animals and plants in everyday life. There can be no doubt that he loved them. A man who would have looked upon them just as an interesting, perhaps admirable, but yet inferior creation, deprived of a soul of the same nature as our own, would have been incapable of writing the two hymns of which the authorship is ascribed, with practical certainty, to the young founder of the Religion of the Disk. A painting in which he is portrayed, as usually, in the midst of his family, shows one of the little princesses fondly stroking the head of a tame gazelle which her sister is holding in her arms—a scene which would suggest, to say the least, that pets were welcome in the palace and that the king's children were actually brought up to love dumb creatures. Budge (1923: 92), moreover, tells us that "not only was the king no warrior, he was not even a lover of the chase," a statement which is confirmed by the fact that not a single hunting scene, not a single inscription set up in commemoration of a successful chase has yet been discovered in the amount of pictorial and written evidence dating from his reign.

And, while waiting for some more decisive proof before giving the question a final answer, one may wonder if the action of pursuing and killing beautiful wild beasts and birds for the sake of sport was not forbidden by him who sang the joy of life in all nature—or at least if he had not expressed for that sort of amusement a sufficient repulsion for his courtiers to refrain from indulging in it, throughout his reign. Such a disgust on his part would be fully in keeping with the spirit of the Religion of the Disk as revealed to us in the hymns.

The absence of records, or the state in which the existing documents have reached us, makes it difficult for one to say anything more about the application to the king's daily life of that principle of truly universal love and brotherhood, surely implied in what we know of his religion. The paintings that portray him eating and drinking have not come down to us sufficiently well preserved for one to assert, without his imagination playing a great part in the guess, which were the items of the royal menu.

The same thing can be said of the piles of offerings heaped upon the altar of the Sun in many a picture where the king and queen are portrayed worshipping. It is hard to make out what they represent, without a great amount of imagination. No scenes actually picturing animal sacrifices have so far been discovered, and the mere presence of bulls garlanded with flowers among the crowd that comes forth to receive the Pharaoh at the entrance of the temple of Aten, on the walls of the tomb of Merira, the High-priest, does not suffice to indicate that those creatures were destined to be slain in some solemn oblation.

Nor can the fact that living victims, "both animal and human," were offered to Re in the temples built by the kings of the Fifth Dynasty throw any light on the sacrificial rituals of the Religion of the Disk. Akhenaten did aim at a revival of very old ideas concerning the Sun, and the well-known connection of his cult with that in the most ancient centre of solar worship—the sacred city of Heliopolis—goes to support that view, no less than the strange archaisms in art that I have pointed out. But that does not mean that he accepted the old ritual as it had once been in use. We know that, merely by forbidding to make any image of his God, he suppressed a number of rites that had been essential in the cult of all the old gods of Egypt. What, exactly, he did away with, and what he kept of the past is not known. The only indication of living creatures being offered to Aten is to be found in the first inscription commemorating the foundation of Akhet-aten. There, along with bread, beer, wine, herbs, fruits, flowers, incense and gold, geese, etc., are mentioned among the items offered at the ceremony which solemnised the consecration of the City's territory. Curiously enough, in the second foundation inscription the enumeration is omitted.

It is stated also that the "hills, deserts, fowl, people, cattle, all things which Aten produced and on which His rays shine" are consecrated to Him by the king, the founder of the city; that "they are all offered to His spirit." Were the geese and other living creatures enumerated in the first inscription selected simply so that the animal as well as the vegetable and mineral world might be represented in the ceremony, and "offered to the spirit of the Sun" in the same manner as the whole territory of the future city with all its inhabitants? Or were they actually destroyed according to the age-old custom? And if the traditional rites of sacrifice were observed on that solemn occasion, were they also a part of the daily worship of Aten in the new capital? One can answer neither of these questions with absolute certainty. Weigall believes that

> the ceremonial side of the religion does not seem to have been complex. The priests, of whom there were very few, offered sacrifices consisting mostly of vegetables, fruits and flowers, to the Aten, and at those ceremonies the king and his family often officiated. They sang psalms and offered prayers, and with much sweet music gave praise to the great Father of joy, and love. (1922: 108)

On the other hand, Budge tells us plainly that "we know nothing of the forms and ceremonies of the Aten worship," but that "hymns and songs and choruses must have filled the temple daily"—the only thing that can be asserted about the external side of the Religion of the Disk, without much risk of being mistaken.

FIRST PROPHET OF A NEW ORDER

But even if one supposes that, at least up to the period of the foundation of Akhet-aten, and maybe also afterwards, some oblations of living creatures were made to the father of life, that would throw very little light on Akhenaten's personal attitude towards beasts and birds. It would, anyhow, in no way disprove the belief in the brotherhood of all creatures which we have attributed to him on the basis of the hymns he composed.

Blood sacrifices, so common in the ancient world, shock the modern man not because they imply a murderous violence—worse cruelties take place today, everywhere, in the name of food, dress, amusement and scientific research—but because the modern man fails to put himself in the place of those who once offered them. He cannot realize what they represented to the minds of those people; he does not understand their meaning. We know that many interpretations of sacrifice can be given, some of which are purely practical, but some of which also, on the contrary, involve an idea of disinterested gift to God; a useless gift of what belongs to Him already, one might say, but still a gift which the worshipper offers in a spirit of sole devotion. Viewed in that particular light, a blood sacrifice, notwithstanding the gruesome action it supposes, is infinitely less repulsive than the equally or more cruel things that the modern man tolerates or encourages: butchery, hunting, harpooning of whales, and scientific experiments at the expense of sentient creatures. It does not stress the difference between man and beast, nor does it imply the childish and barbaric dogma that beasts have been created for man to exploit at his convenience. It does not sever the tie of brotherhood between the offerer and the victim.

Whatever may have been the ritual in the temples of Akhet-aten, there is one fact which invites us to believe that Akhenaten strongly stressed, in his teaching and by his behavior, that all living creatures are our brothers through the Sun, our common Father. This is the definite mention, in the inscription on the first boundary-stone of the sacred city, of the solemn burial of the bull Mnevis in a tomb in the eastern hills, near the king's own sepulcher and those of his nobles. "And the sepulcher of Mnevis shall be made in the eastern hills, and he shall be buried therein."

Mnevis was the sacred bull symbolizing the Sun incarnate in the eyes of the priests of Heliopolis. By giving him a worthy place of rest in the cemetery of his new capital, the Pharaoh, no doubt, wished to point out the filiations of his cult to that which was perhaps the oldest form of Sun-worship in Egypt, and thereby to impress in its favor a nation naturally inclined to cling to tradition. But there surely was more than that in his gesture. Akhenaten, who cared so little for success, would not, it seems, have done anything simply for the sake of policy. There must have been some deeper religious significance attached to the honors rendered to the old bull, apart from his being the holy animal. The Religion of the Disk was, after all, something quite distinct from the archaic cult of the Sun, though it had its roots in it.

What was this religious significance is nowhere stated. But if we bear in mind the spirit of the hymns, in which man, beast, bird, fish and plant are shown in turn to be the objects of the one God's impartial solicitude, and, each one to the capacity of its nature, His worshippers, then it seems quite possible that Akhenaten desired to honor the bull Mnevis less as the sacred bull of Heliopolis, traditional symbol of vigor and fertility, than as an individual beast standing for Animality in general, the mother of humanity. It stood for the sacred realm of life, of which human reason is only a late aspect and the clear knowledge of truth the ultimate flower. By the special treatment he gave him, he might well have wished to remind his followers both of the kindness that man should show to all living beings—his brothers—and of the respect he should feel for the great forces of life at play within their dumb consciousness, more frankly and more innocently than in his own.

The inscriptions dating from the time of the great reaction against Akhenaten's work emphasize the decay in which the shrines of the gods and their estates had fallen, during his reign, through neglect. "The sanctuaries were overthrown and the sacred sites had become thoroughfares for the people," states the well-known stele of Tutankhamen in Cairo. It is remarkable that not a word is said about what happened to the sacred beasts—crocodiles, ibis, ichneumons, cats, etc.—that formed such a striking feature in the cult of the local gods. A real "religious fanatic," enemy of the gods and of all that was connected with them, would probably have had those animals destroyed as living idols.

But Akhenaten did nothing of the kind, or his enemies would not have omitted to mention it with pious indignation. Not only had he had no quarrel with the living beings which human veneration had set apart as sacred, but perhaps even did he believe that, in the superstition to which they owed such unusual attention, there lay a solid kernel of truth. Whatever might have been the primitive state of religion with which their worship was linked, in the eyes of the mob, they perhaps appeared, in his eyes, as reminders of that great truth, centre of the real religion expounded in his own hymns, namely of the oneness of all life and of the brotherhood of man and beast, united in the common worship of their common maker, father and mother—"the Heat which-is-in-the-Disk." The silence of Amun's scribes on their fate during the young Pharaoh's reign inclines us to believe that they did appear as such to him. Thanks to his orders, they lacked neither the food nor the care that they were accustomed to enjoy.

This instance, along with the general tone of the hymns, strengthens our conviction that there was a religious meaning in the royal honors given to the Bull of Heliopolis—the Beast of the Sun, that stood for all the sacred animals, perhaps as the most ancient, surely as the most exalted of them all; a religious meaning which was none other than that which we have tried to make clear.

If that be so, then one should consider Akhenaten not merely as the oldest exponent of the rationalism of our age, the first man to stress the scientific basis of true universal religion, but also as the forerunner of a world far more beautiful and better than our own. Even more: as the first prophet of a new order in which not only would there be no distinction between one's countrymen and foreigners, but in which the same loving kindness would extend alike to man and to all living creatures.

In fact, I firmly hold that, unless and until man learns to love his animal brothers as himself, and to respect them, as children and worshippers of the same Father of all life, he will not be able to live at peace with his own species. He must deserve peace before he can enjoy it. And no society which tolerates the shameful exploitation of sentient creatures that cannot retaliate, deserves to remain, itself, unmolested by its stronger, shrewder, and better-equipped human neighbors.

If Akhenaten's "internationalism" and "pacifism" were but a consequence of the broader and more fundamental principle of the brotherhood of living creatures; if his love towards all men proceeded from a deeper love towards all life, then one must hail in him perhaps the most ancient exponent of integral truth. And at the same time, as one whose spirit the modern world seems still unable to understand—one from whom the yet unborn generations would do well to learn the way of life.

Fig. 8: Akhenaten and family enjoy the bounty of the Aten.

CHAPTER 7

THE WAY OF BEAUTY

I have tried up till now to show, in the Religion of the Disk, the rare combination of rationalism and love which one seeks in vain in most revealed faiths of later times. And we have seen, in its youthful Founder, that alliance of intellectual genius and of saintliness, perhaps still more rarely witnessed at any epoch in the same individual. A closer study of the hymns and of whatever other evidence is available will further stress that, in him, both the lofty rational thinker and the lover of all life were expressions of the all-round artist. The keynote of that particular form of Sun-worship which he evolved lay in an intense sense of beauty.

The hymns are, before all, songs of praise exalting the beauty of the visible Sun, the splendor of light. "Thou art sparkling; Thou art beautiful and mighty... Thy light of diverse colors bewitcheth all faces"; "Thou vivifiest hearts with Thy beauties which are life," it is said in the shorter hymn. And in the longer hymn, common are the sentences in the same trend that magnify the Disk in heaven as lovely to look upon:

> Thy rising is beautiful in the horizon of heaven, O Aten, ordainer of life... Thou fillest every land with Thy beauty... Thou art beautiful and great and sparkling and exalted above every land.... Thou art afar off; but Thy beams are upon the earth; Thou art in their faces; they admire Thy goings... [C]reatures live through Thee, while their eyes are upon Thy beauty.

And not only are such expressions applied to the Sun Himself, but the whole picture of the world pulsating with life and joy under His daily touch—men, bathed and clothed in clean garments, raising their hands in adoration to Him. Birds circled round with thrills of joy in the clear morning sky. Beasts ran and skipped about in fields flooded with light. Fishes, whose golden scales shine through the sunlit water, leapt up from the depth, before the rising God. And the tender lilies opened themselves to His fiery kiss and "drink themselves drunk" of warmth, of light, of impalpable brilliance, in the marshes where they bloom—that entire picture is the inspired vision of an artist which, more than anything else, Akhenaten was.

No less than the perfection of the one God, the hymns exalt the joy of life and the loveliness of the visible world. Life is sweet, in fact, because there is so much beauty all round us. It is a pleasure to have eyes and to behold graceful forms and delicate colors—the green trees and water-reeds, the rich brown earth, the reddish-yellow desert, the blue hills in the distance and, above all, the deep, transparent, boundless, radiant sky, with the flaming orb— "rising, shining, departing afar off and returning"; to witness the glory of dawn and sunset. It is a pleasure to see happy four-legged creatures stretch out their bodies in the light. It is a pleasure to see a flight of birds sail through the calm, vibrating infinity. It is a pleasure to listen to the noises of life: the song of the crickets, children's laughter, and the music of the wind in the high trees. It is a pleasure to be alive, for there is beauty in the child, in the beast, in the bird, in the trees—in all that lives. Beauty in land, water and sky—in all that is. The emphasis that the young Pharaoh puts on the ravishment of the senses at the sight of daylight is perhaps equaled only in the masterpieces of Greek literature, centuries later. It forestalls the words so often repeated by the chorus in classical tragedies: "It is sweet to behold the Sun."

PERFECTION ON EARTH

One can say of Akhenaten's whole life that it was an attempt to establish on this earth, here and now, the reign of perfection. His city, as we have seen previously, was to be the city of God, the model of that ideal world which he visualized in his heart and which seems to us, still today, so far, far away, so unreal, so impossible. And it was "a place of surpassing beauty," planned "with delicate taste and supreme elegance."

I have already spoken of its temples with their successive pillared courts open to the sky; of its fair villas surrounded with palm-groves and flower-beds; of the king's palace, that exceeded in splendor that in which Amenhotep III had spent in Thebes his luxurious days; and of the peaceful gardens that lay to the south, with their colonnaded pavilions, their verdant arbors, their artificial lakes full of lotuses. The elegant architecture of the houses and villas, of the palace and temples—the sober outlines of light-colored brick against a clear sky; the harmonious perspectives of pillared porticos and inner halls, with deep contrasts of light and shadow; and the airy splendor of the sacred courts with their single altar smoking under the bright sunshine, on a flight of steps—that architecture, we say, was in tune with its natural setting. And the fresh, shady gardens in the neighborhood of the desert seemed all the more fresh and delightful; and the reddish-yellow sands in the background all the more austere, all the more end-less and barren—full of sunshine alone; full of infinite peace. The city was not, as are so many others, a monument of man's domination over nature, and of his pride. It was but a beautiful detail added to the immense landscape, as a permanent offering to the soul of all beings, the Sun. It was a monument of worship lying between the silent sands, the majestic river, and the radiant sky.

But it is not only in the emphasis he put in his hymns on the beauty of the Sun-disk; not only in the choice of an inspiring site and in the building of "as fair a city as the world had ever seen" that Akhenaten proves himself an artist in the full sense of the word. The arts held a large place both in his cult and in his life. As far as one can tell from the paintings and reliefs that depict him in familiar attitudes, his days were works of beauty.

As already said, we know hardly anything about the ceremonial of the Religion of the Disk; but we do know that music and singing—and dancing—were an essential part of it. It is written in the shorter hymn that "singing men and singing women and chorus men produce joyful sounds in the Hall of the House of the Benben Obelisk, and in every temple of Akhet-aten, the seat of Truth." In a painting in the tomb of the high-priest Merira, that represents a visit of the king and queen to the main temple of Aten, probably on a festive occasion, one can see a group of blind musicians singing to the accompaniment of a seven-stringed harp. And this is not the only pictorial evidence of musical instruments used in the temples to glorify the one God. Moreover, from the famous stele in which Tutankhamen describes the state of Egypt under the "heretic" Pharaoh, it appears that Akhenaten also maintained a large number of dancers in connection with the service of Aten.

We know, too, that the places of worship which he dedicated, be it in Thebes during the first years of his reign, be it in his sacred city, were richly adorned with frescoes and bas-reliefs and statues. The temple built as Queen Tiye's private house of worship, on the occasion of her coming to Akhet-aten, and named "Shade of the Sun," contained statues of the king himself, of Amenhotep III, and of the dowager-queen, between the columns that stood on either side of its main court. There were statues of the royal couple—or perhaps of Akhenaten with one of his daughters—in front of each column at the entrance of the pillared portico which led into the smaller temple of Aten. And it is highly probable that, in the shrines dedicated to the memory of the king's father and to that of his ancestors, Thotmose IV, Amenhotep II, etc., statues of those monarchs were to be seen as well as diverse representations of them in color and relief.

This shows that, rigorously monotheistic as it surely was, the Religion of the Disk remained a religion strongly appealing to the senses; one that readily put to contribution all manner of artistic skill, and gave occasion to the greatest display of beauty. Men and women attached to the temples praised the "Lord and Origin of life" in solos and choruses, and on the harp. Sistrums were rattled and drums beaten at certain solemn moments during the ceremonies. And, no doubt also to the accompaniment of music, sacred dancers expressed, in symbolical attitudes and harmoniously suggestive movements, the succession of the seasons or the daily course of the Sun. Akhenaten, so vehemently opposed to any graven or painted representation of God, did not object in the least to the presence in temples of statues of human beings whom he wished to honor, or of fanciful figures, semi-animal, semi-human, such as that remarkable sphinx *en relief* in his own likeness, familiar to all students of the Tell-el-Amarna art. Any image of God, already sacrilegious in itself by its necessary inadequacy, could tempt the worshipper to forget the Unnameable and Limitless, and to carry his homage to the concrete shape. It was a lie and a danger.

While in the portraits in color or in stone of people destined to be exalted, but not adored, there lay no such falsehood and no such snare. The Pharaoh not only tolerated them, but seems to have encouraged his sculptors to produce them, for the embellishment of the "Houses of Aten." Perhaps, also, did he expect to strengthen the faith of his followers by maintaining them in contact with the long tradition of Egyptian Sun-worship, of which the upstart cult of Amun was, in his eyes, a distortion, and his own teaching the culmination. That worship had been linked, in the minds of the people, with a religious reverence for the monarch and his line. The fact was not one to be disdained.

Be it so or otherwise, Akhenaten evidently looked upon melodious sounds and rhythmic movements, and colors and forms pleasing to the eye, as powerful means of edification. And he closely associated his rational cult with all the arts. Nothing was more alien to his spirit than that austere Puritanism, enemy of dance and music, which so many zealous reformers of various creeds put forward centuries after him, apparently with the purpose of turning the hearts of the faithful away from the world back to God. To him, the visible beauty of the world was god-like; the refined joys of the senses were uplifting to the soul. And the latter-day idea of the opposition of "the world" to God would have seemed to him impious and absurd.

What perhaps characterizes Akhenaten the best, besides his uncompromising truthfulness, is the atmosphere of serene beauty in which he seems to have moved in daily life. We have sufficiently stressed the quiet splendor of his material surroundings, the place of the arts in his leisure, and his constant contact with nature, not to have to insist on those points here too elaborately. Yet we cannot help recalling the sets of reliefs in the tomb of Huya which represent the royal family and the dowager-queen feasting, while two string bands play alternately. One of the musical groups consists of "four female performers, the one playing on a harp, the second and third on a lute, and the fourth on a lyre," while in the other can be distinguished "a large standing lyre, about six feet in height, having eight strings and being played with both hands" (Weigall 1922: 156-157).

Here we have one more instance of Akhenaten's love of every form of sensuous beauty. Both the loveliness of nature and the fine arts were to him a part and parcel of ordinary life no less than of the temple services. They produced something like a rhythmic accompaniment to the simple gestures that we repeat every day; a background on which the most monotonous actions took on a decorous beauty. The sweet-smelling freshness of those pillars festooned with flowers and green leaves, the sight of fair figures and harmonious movements, the soft music, the elegant shape of the cup as well as the taste of the good rich wine, all combined to raise that most ordinary act of quenching his thirst to the level of a higher enjoyment involving the whole being—a moment of beauty. Life was to be a succession of such moments to anyone who, like him, lived it in a spirit of sincerity, of innocence and of understanding. To anyone, that is to say, who knew the value of simple things—of a fiery reflection upon the wall, of a sweet voice, of a child's smile—as well as of the so-called great ones, and who could constantly feel the presence of the divine Disk, with His rays stretched over the world, "encompassing all lands which He made," beautifying, dignifying, sanctifying the humblest manifestations of everyday existence.

The things which, in our age of specialized activities might appear as trifles when connected with the life of a philosopher and of a prophet, did not seem so to him. From the pictures we have of him, it is visible that he brought in the care of his person, and particularly of his dress, an eagerness that numbers of later saintly teachers would have disdained. Not only was he scrupulously clean, but he knew what to wear, and how to wear it. The exquisite painted relief in the Berlin Museum, in which one sees him smelling a bunch of flowers, and the picture in the tomb of Merira which shows him burning perfumes at the altar of the Sun, speak eloquently of the supreme elegance of his attire. Save on very special occasions, he seems to have discarded the abundant display of jewels customary to other Pharaohs, and in those two pictures, as in many others, he is portrayed wearing none at all. His only ornaments are the soft pleats of his garment itself—a simple white skirt of fine linen, that hangs gracefully from the waist, with a long purple sash. And the garment seems to have no other function but to underline the natural grace of the body.

Commenting upon the portrait in the Berlin Museum just referred to, Hall (1936: 305) rightly remarks that there is in it a delicacy only to be found in the best productions of Greek sculpture. We may add that Akhenaten's passionate love of tangible beauty, of sunshine and of healthy joy, such as it is expressed both in his poems, in his cult and in his person, makes him the first illustrious individual embodiment of that very ideal of art and life which the Hellenes were to put forward, as a nation, a thousand years after him.

AN AESTHETIC OF LIGHT

A lover of sensuous beauty Akhenaten was indeed, and to the utmost. But he did not stop there. From the happy awareness of color, line and movement, of touch, of sound, of fragrance, he lifted himself, as we know, to the subtler plane of abstract relations and finally to the realization of the all-pervading oneness of the supreme entity: the Power within the Sun.

We need not here expound on the great principles on which his creed was based, principles of which modern science has confirmed the amazing accuracy: the ultimate equivalence of all forms of energy, and the ultimate identity of energy and matter. As most if not all ideas of genius, these appear to have resulted from some direct insight into truth, which it is not possible to account for either by the data of external experience available at the time, or by the ordinary means of discursive reasoning. And what the hymns tell us plainly, and what the pictures suggest to us of Akhenaten's extreme sensitiveness to beauty, makes us think of the fundamental connection between scientific enlightenment and artistic inspiration, put forward so forcefully nowadays in autobiographical essays, by eminent creative scientists.

The knowledge which the Pharaoh expressed by calling the "Lord of Rays" also "Great One of roarings" (or thunders) and by identifying the "Heat-and-light-within-the-Disk" with the Disk itself, came to him, it would seem, as all great ideas do to their discoverers, namely, through some spontaneous intuition following a long period of subconscious preparation. And if, in most cases, the aesthetic element plays a notable part in the discovery of truth; if a particular solution of a mathematical problem, or a particular explanation of physical data, seems to draw the mind to it by its very simplicity and elegance, then we can all the more safely conjecture that the young author of the hymns and inspirer of the Tell-el-Amarna school of art was urged to put forth his hypothesis of universal oneness. He did so for the beauty of the endless horizons it opened to his vision; for the impressive harmony it brought into his conception of things.

His preparation was that very quest for the perfect that appears to have possessed him all his life, the "perfect" being, in his eyes, primarily, that which would totally satisfy his aesthetic sense: flawless beauty. And the consciousness of the unity of all forms of energy in the intangible soul of the Sun seems to have come to him as the sharp, direct feeling of a perfect pattern, half-hidden by the necessary limitations of material existence. It was the vision of an immense orderly scheme, remarkable by its stately simplicity; the product of his own mind, no doubt, but destined, one day, to prove objective. It was, actually, the vision of the permanent underlying beauty of the universe, to which an all-round artist could alone have access.

Thus Akhenaten loved the world of forms because it is beautiful, and, through it, soon grasped and loved the eternal beauty of the unseen world of essences. The splendor of the Disk that rises and sets led him to the worship of the "Ka" of the Disk, the supreme essence. When, a thousand years later, Plato put forward his famous dialective of love, he expressed nothing else but that which the youthful Founder of the Religion of the Disk had once realized, lived, and taught.

ONENESS AND BEAUTY

Not only does the king's insight into the nature of the physical world seem to spring mainly from an innate yearning for the beautiful, but his belief in the oneness of life has apparently the same origin.

The hymns tell the beauty of the Sun and the joy of all creatures at His sight. The works of the Tell-el-Amarna school show us what the beauty of creatures meant both to the disciples and to the master. The happy scenes of animal and plant life, such as, for instance, those depicted on the pavements of the king's palace, have more than a decorative value. They preach the love of living beings for the sake of that beauty which shines in even the meanest among them. They remind us what a masterpiece of the supreme artist is a quadruped, or a butterfly; a poppy; even a blade of grass. And they prompt us to love the graceful innocent things which only wish to live and enjoy the day-light: the young calf frisking in the sunshine, the wild geese, the fish that leap up from the depth to greet the Sun, the spotless lilies.

As I have already stressed, Akhenaten's conscientious objection to war which brought both the end of Egyptian domination in Syria and, indirectly, the downfall of the cult of Aten in Egypt, seems to have been but one aspect of his objection to the infliction of suffering in general. And in the light of all that we know of him through his poems, we may safely say that the main source of his love for living beings, from man to plant, and the main reason for him to wish to spare them, lay in his intense awareness of the beauty of life as such. He saw in every sentient creature, patiently brought forth from an obscure germ by the action of divine heat and light and graced with all the loveliness of its species, a work of art far too precious to be destroyed or spoilt for the sake of sport or vain glory. And that is apparently why we find, during his reign, neither records of chase nor accounts of battle.

It would seem that he had little time for such "grim beauty" as painters and poets have sometimes tried to bring out of scenes of horror. And that con-firms our view that visible beauty, however important in his eyes, was not all to him. Beyond it—and through it—he sought that permanent harmony between fact and thought, action and ideal, existence and essence; that subtler beauty which cannot be discovered from a superficial view of things, and which is the essence of goodness. A scene of horror can only be beautiful seen in its outlines or from a distance. Once one stoops to examine the details that go to make it, one finds that it implies too much ugliness to be described as such. Nothing which presupposes the distortion of living forms through pain can be styled as beautiful. In healthy sentient life lies the actual masterpiece of universal energy and the supreme beauty.

Here we may remark that, for Akhenaten as for the greatest artist among Greek philosophers, more than ten centuries after him, the Beautiful and the Good were closely interrelated, if not identical. But instead of saying, as Plato was to do, that "the Beautiful is the radiance of the Good," that the young Prophet of the Sun would have said that the Good is that which is consistently beautiful. Strictly speaking, it is correct to assert, with several modern authors, that there is no reference to morality in Akhenaten's teaching and that, to him, 'that which is' was right.

On the other hand, it would be unfair to the Religion of the Disk not to admit that, though it put forth no list of commandments and prohibitions, it had nevertheless a close connection with action. And the practical side of it appears to have rested entirely upon an aesthetic basis. Moral values were, to Akhenaten, but the highest among aesthetic values. In other words, beauty was the ultimate criterion of moral as well as of intellectual truth, and the safest guide to the discovery of both.

A RELIGION OF BEAUTY

We can thus characterize the Religion of the Disk as a *religion of beauty*. Whatever it be in addition to that, springs from that fundamental aspect of it. In particular, its three negative features which we have pointed out in a previous chapter—namely, the absence in it of any mythology whatsoever; the absence of any account of supernatural happenings; and the absence of any explicit theory of the next world—seem partly ascribable to a consistently "pagan" spirit. Mythological symbolism was superfluous. The facts of the physical world were beautiful enough to stand at the background of any solemn cult and to inspire any sensitive soul. Nature was beautiful enough, without man craving for the supernatural. And this life, here and now, was beautiful enough for one to live it with all one's concentrated interest, drawing from it its daily joys and its daily teachings, without seeking to pierce the mystery of the great beyond.

There is much more in the hymns than a mere physical enjoyment of the Sun. But a thrill of well-being at the contact of light, of warmth and of happy living nature; a feeling of plenitude at the sight of the loveliness of the visible world is surely there, at the root of all subsequent idealism. The repeated praise of the sweetness of sunshine; the choice of expressions that suggest, in the most various creatures, an exaltation of all their being at the appearing of the Sun; the predominant idea of universal fecundity, expressed in different pictures of appealing beauty; all go to confirm that essentially pagan joy which I have mentioned above. I use here the word "pagan" in its noblest sense, suggesting thereby how much the inspired king stands as an upholder of that ideal of healthy, joyful, sensuous perfection—and also of clear rational thinking—towards which Greece and the whole Mediterranean world have strived, long after him, in their days of glory. He appears to us, nay, as the historic forerunner of classical Hellas.

The love implied in his songs is not that unjustified interest in our species before all others, preached by most of the creeds which have transcended the national and mainly ritualistic religions of antiquity. It springs from the consciousness of the brotherhood of all beings to whom the Sun gives life and loveliness. It is the truly universal love in the light of which the superstition of the chosen species appears as puerile and barbaric as that of the chosen nation. It is the love for the beast, the fish, the plant, no less than for man, clearly put forward by none of the living religions of the world save a few of those evolved in India. But while, in those doctrines, such love seems based upon metaphysical considerations or upon moral principles, it appears to be, in the Religion of the Disk, the immediate spontaneous outcome of an overwhelming sense of the beauty of life. If indeed beauty be the final measure of all values, then surely man is not the centre of the universe and the focus of all desirable activity. The other children of the life-giving God are as lovely as he, if not more, in their absolute innocence.

The Glory of Light

Ever since the bitter struggle between the eminently artistic and rational spirit of Hellenism and eminently humanitarian Christianity, in the early centuries of the western era, the best minds of the West have been yearning for the synthesis which would unite the excellences of the complementary wisdoms. Possibly also, in other areas of culture, the need of a similar synthesis has been experienced between old thought-currents, each one expressing separately the everlasting ideals of aesthetic perfection, of intellectual efficiency and of kindness that knows no limits.

The Religion of the Disk, with its joyous intoxication of sunshine and tangible beauty, seems to provide an answer to the age-long yearning for something that would satisfy all sides of our nature at the same time. The inspiration that fills it is perhaps of the only sort that can lift us to heaven without detaching us from this lovely and lovable earth. And whatever be one's opinion of him on other points, one has to admit that we do find combined in its founder the best of the ideal Athenian, more than a thousand years before Plato, and the best of the ideal Indian, some nine centuries before the Buddha.

Fig. 9: Akhenaten seated.

CHAPTER 8

IMPLICATIONS OF THE RELIGION OF THE DISK

One of the most frequent criticisms brought against the Religion of the Disk by modern authors is that it is devoid of the sense of righteousness. Budge writes plainly that "no consciousness of sin is expressed in any Aten text now known, and the hymns to Aten contain no petition for spiritual enlightenment, understanding or wisdom." In another passage, after comparing Aten to Varuna as described in the Rig-Veda, he adds: "But Varuna possessed one attribute which, so far as we know, is wanting in the Aten: he spied out sin, and judged the sinner" (1923: 114). And Breasted, though he admires the teaching, tells us that

> our surviving sources for the Aten faith do not disclose a very
> spiritual conception of the deity, nor any attribution to him of
> ethical qualities beyond those which Re had long been supposed
> to possess. Our sources do not show us that the king had percep-
> tibly risen from a discernment of the beneficence to a conception
> of the righteousness in the character of God, nor of His demand
> for this in the character of men. (1924: 120).

There is hardly anyone but Petrie and Weigall who seem fully to appreciate the "great change" which marks Akhenaten's reign "in ethics also," and to recognize the practical value of the teaching put forward in the hymns, in the tomb inscriptions of Tell-el-Amarna, and in the luminous instance of Akhenaten's life as a ruler and as a man.

Yet even Weigall, when comparing the Religion of the Disk with Christianity, is prompted to state that "this comparison must of necessity be unfavorable to the Pharaoh's creed, revealing, as it does, its shortcomings" (1922: 127). This opinion, so entirely different from mine, springs eventually from that idea, more strongly expressed by other authors, that the *consciousness of evil* is lacking in the Religion of Aten.

It is a fact that in the existing documents relating to the teaching, there is no exhaustive list of commandments and prohibitions, no precise rules—no rules at all—for the guidance of the disciple's life, such as one finds in the sacred books of most religions. There is no mention of a distributive Justice, and it is possible, even probable, that Akhenaten disbelieved "in the dogma of rewards for the righteous and punishments for the evil-doers" (Budge 1923: 95). There is, indeed, nowhere the slightest hint at the existence of a positive power of evil, age-old antagonist of a beneficent God and master of deceit, as the Satan of the Bible. Nowhere is there the slightest awareness of what later ethical religions have styled as "sin"—*i.e.*, the transgression of God's orders.

Akhenaten's God gave no orders. He is an "amoral" God. We must remember that He is not a man; nor a being superior to man who made man in his likeness. He is the immanent power within all things; the source of life—not a person; the one indefinable principle that burns in heat, shines in light, roars and sings in sound, moves through matter as electricity; the principle that exists at the root of the ultimate unity of existence. Can such a God be reduced to our petty standards? Can He be "good" or "bad" at our scale? —be "moral" or "immoral"? No immanent God can be. To no God who bears to the physical universe the intimate relation which Akhenaten's "Shu-within-the-Disk" bears to it, can be ascribed a moral personality. His consciousness, if any, is not a personal one. His love for His creatures is as indiscriminate as the warmth of the Sun-beams, that radiate both over the good and over the wicked. The idea of a distributive justice is a human idea—not God's concern. Morality is in us; not in Him.

LIVING IN TRUTH

Should then a follower of Akhenaten take the easy course of doing just what he pleases?

The founder of the Religion of the Disk insisted upon "life in truth." "There is in his teaching, as it is fragmentarily preserved in his hymns and in the tomb-inscriptions of his nobles, a constant emphasis upon 'truth' such as is not found before or since," says Breasted. He called himself "*Ankh-em-Maat*"—"the One-who-lives-in-Truth." But what is truth? "Maat," writes Budge (1923: 86), "means what is straight, true, real, law, both physical and moral, the truth, reality, etc." By "living in truth" the king

> can hardly have meant 'living in or by the law,' for he was a law
> to himself. But he may have meant that in Atenism he had found
> the truth or the 'real' thing, and that all else, in religion, was a
> phantom, a sham. Aten lived in Maat, or in truth and reality, and
> the king, having the essence of Aten in him, did the same.

If this interpretation of Maat be the right one, then it appears that a man's behavior should be, in Akhenaten's eyes, inspired by the knowledge of the few facts and the acceptance of the few supreme values which form the solid background of the Aten faith. They were the few general truths which modern research is gradually confirming, and which would still satisfy, it seems, the thinking men of the remotest ages to come. The Religion was the only true religion, and "all but it was a phantom, a sham," in the sense that it was not a particular creed, with undeniable religious appeal but, also, with necessary limitations destined to become more and more apparent as centuries would pass. It was not a religion among many, but the framework from which no teaching could seriously depart if it was to be absolutely universal, and to stand victoriously the test of time. It set forth no commandments. It had no catalogue of "dos" and "don'ts." Yet it could be, and was, a guide to behavior, for the reason that our behavior is the outcome of what we are—that is to say, of what we know and of what we love.

The Religion of the Disk was based upon the intuitive knowledge of this harmonious universe, dominated (at our scale at least) by the Sun, our "Father and Mother," and upon the love of its beauty. He who possessed these needed no commandments in order to live according to the master's standards—in harmony with the beautiful world, in harmony with life, with his own deeper nature; "in truth."

The visible universe obeys laws—those great cosmic laws, of whatever nature they be, that bring into it that majestic order of which the trained human mind can catch a glimpse; the laws that rule the course of the stars and the play of matter. The invisible world, likewise, has its laws of action and reaction, no less true. He who wishes to "live in truth" should not only think of those divine unwritten laws "both physical and moral," and act rationally, in small things as well as in great ones, but strive to reflect the beauty of the sunlit earth and the impartial kindness of the power within the Sun. He should love all creatures as himself—as He loves them, whose rays cause them to live. He should do no harm to them under any pretext. Injury to the humblest beast or bird, on the part of a rational being who should know better, is an insult to the Lord of life, a sacrilege. But that is not enough. He should help them to live and to be happy; to enjoy the light and heat of the common father and render praise to Him, each one in the manner of its species. He can only be fully rational if he be actively loving, and beneficent to all that lives, as Akhenaten himself appears to have been.

One must remark that this faithfulness to a divine pattern, this feeling of the beauty and importance of life, this active, impartial beneficence were not ordered by the young king as befitting a true follower of his teaching. They were part and parcel of the personality of whoever was fit to be a disciple. And the teaching was wasted upon those who, by nature, did not possess a suffi-cient sensitiveness and a sufficient intelligence to be already inclined that way. This is perhaps one of the reasons why Akhenaten seems to have actually preached his doctrine only to a very few people. By the nature of the worship it involved, the Religion of the Disk was suitable to all creatures, from the superman down to the sunflower. But in its practical implications it supposed such a degree of inborn refinement that, far from being applicable to all men, it was, and probably will always remain, a teaching for the elite. Its morality, essentially aesthetic, and therefore aristocratic, was too free and too generous for the many to understand—a reason why the Aten faith has so often been characterized in our times as entirely "amoral."

There appears to be some ambiguity about the word "morality." What commonly passes off as such would be better described as obedience to the rules of some definite society at a definite stage of development; to police reg-ulations in the broader sense. According to that popular conception, what one *does* is more important than what one *is*; what one is only matters inasmuch as it cannot but determine what one thinks and feels, and ultimately what one does, when left to one's self. And what one has to do or not to do is decided by the requirements of the community to which one belongs. In all successful religions, the list of "moral" commandments and prohibitions is intimately linked up with the idea of community, of society. And its practical stability depends upon its susceptibility of receiving various interpretations as the con-ception of society changes with time and place. Its aim is mainly to make each one of the faithful the worthy member of a human group, or of several broad-ening human groups—family, tribe or caste, nation, race, humanity.

In the Religion of the Disk, there was no such conception of gregarious obligations. It was not a religion fitting the members of any particular group at any particular epoch. It was the teaching suited to the fully-conscious indi-vidual, in love with the beauty of the Sun and aware, through Him, of his per-sonal relationship to the whole of living creation. The fully-conscious indi-vidual has transcended the bondage of all arbitrary communities. He is actu-ally the member of no group, save of the totality of sentient individuals of all races and species. He owes allegiance to the father of life alone. He fulfils the "duties" that other men recognize towards their narrow groups, but not for the same reasons nor in the same spirit as they. Whenever those duties do not clash with the broader and more fundamental obligation of love towards all life, he fulfils them, in the very name of that deeper obligation. In other cases he does not look upon them as duties. The natural law of his being is the only law of his conduct. And his conduct is consistent with a norm of inner beauty never approached by any group-regulations, precisely because his being has attained the elegance of natural honesty, natural courage, and natural kindness.

He can do what he pleases, and remain an exponent of reason and of love. Nay, indeed, it is only by acting thus, according to his own law, that he is able to remain so; for love and reason are at the root of his being, and he is aware of it.

Breasted says, in his comment on the meaning of "life in truth," that for Akhenaten "what 'was' was right, and its propriety was evident by its very existence" (1924: 120). Surely the learned historian does not intend to say that, to the young Pharaoh, all that it was the custom to do was right, simply because people did it; still less that, in his eyes, all that a man did was right, just because it had been possible for him to do it. This would be absurd.

The king's life-long struggle against organized superstition, and his strange attitude in front of the political "realities" of his age, prove sufficiently that he did not accept any established tradition as a criterion of right and wrong. And his indignant letter to Aziru, on the murder of one of his most faithful vassals, preserved to posterity in his diplomatic correspondence, shows well that no action became justified on the sole ground of being a fait accompli. To him, all that 'was' in the ordinary sense was not necessarily right. But what was absolutely, in the religious sense; that is to say, what was always and everywhere; what was, in the estimation of the higher conscious-ness, more subtle, more acute, more farseeing than the ordinary—that was right, and that alone.

A Deeper Morality

From the previous remarks we should conclude that though it comprised no particular series of commandments and prohibitions as most other religions do, the Aten faith was far from being without any definite moral implications. For if there be a fundamental difference between genuine morality and glori-fied police regulations, it lies no doubt in the flexibility and freedom of moral actions, compared with those ruled by written law or by custom.

A really moral action is a work of art in which the whole personality of the agent is involved, a creation stamped with individuality. The action resulting from mere obedience to precise imperatives is not. Anybody can blindly move according to well-formulated dictates. It is not up to everyone to reflect the serene beauty of the father of life; to radiate love—*to live in truth*. The actual saints of all religions have consciously or unconsciously striven to do so, while average men have always been impressed by the letter of moral injunctions rather than by their spirit.

The real difference between the Religion of the Disk and most other faiths is that, while the latter have provided strict rules of conduct for every person who wishes to adhere to them, Akhenaten's teaching has not. It merely created an aesthetic atmosphere in which the sensitive soul could easily lift itself towards the everlastingly beautiful, that is both the true and the good. It set forth an object of inspiration such as whoever loved it with all his senses, with all his heart and all his intellect, would automatically be the most virtuous of men. But it did not go down into details, and tell the disciple what to do or not to do in every particular circumstance of his life. That was left to his own ability for grasping moral truth: that is to say, finally, to a sort of aesthetic intuition.

The Religion of the Disk was an expression of the very essence of true religion in the most harmonious language of reason and beauty, rather than a particular creed. It was, as put forward in the famous royal motto, "Living in Truth," the essence of moral life, independent of man-made codes of morals, and freed from the fear of hell-fire no less than from that of human sanctions. Akhenaten gave out no commandments, just as he proclaimed no dogmas. The few who were able to enter the spirit of his teaching needed none. And those who lacked that sort of aesthetic sense which alone enables one to grasp vital cosmic values, would not have been actually "living in truth"—any more than a man with no taste can become an artist just by following all the technical rules of an art.

LOVE AS ETERNAL LIFE

If anything can rouse in a man that yearning to live in harmony with eternal values that dominate him, it is surely not the tedious observance of duties imposed upon him by law or by custom. But it may be the glowing example of a superior individual. All the great teachers of the world seem to have been far greater by the personal example they have set than by the precepts they have left, however sublime these be.

The absence of explicit precepts, easily applicable to every circumstance of life, was perhaps one of the traits of profound rationality which prevented the Aten faith from remaining an organized religion. While the example of its founder stands forever to inspire all those who believe that ceremonial alone should be organized, real religion being essentially personal—and unorganizable. The ethics of the Religion of the Disk were based upon cosmic values. One should add that they were based upon cosmic values as realized by one exceptional man. The historic figure of Akhenaten dominated them even still more, perhaps, than it did the other aspects of the teaching, all of which are inseparable from it.

The one duty which the disciples readily accepted was to imitate him whom they called the "Bright Image of the Sun," the "Son of the Living Aten, like unto Him forever." And that would be the only duty to propose to any man who might wish, in the future, to revive the 3,300-year-old religion of love and reason, and make the young prophet of the Sun a living force in our world. By imitating him I mean not slavishly copying his actions, but imbibing the spirit in which he lived: uncompromising truthfulness, perfect sincerity, allied to the rare courage to stick to what one knows to be right, even at the cost of the highest worldly interests. And along with that, loving kindness, extended to all creatures.

In the tomb of Ay, one finds in an inscription the words: "He" (Akhenaten) "put truth into me, and my abomination is to lie." It is difficult to say, in the light of Ay's subsequent career, how far this assertion was genuine on his part. But it does express the ideal attitude of a disciple of the young king. All wrong, in Akhenaten's eyes, was but a lie under some form or another. The follower of the Religion of the Disk had really but to seek the truth of his deeper self, and to live up to it in full sincerity. The example of the master showed him how beautiful could be the life of a man who did so.

A PANTHEISTIC MONISM

The importance of Akhenaten himself as a living illustration of his teaching cannot be overestimated. He was fully conscious of it when, in his hymns, he gave to posterity such sentences as the following:

- "I am Thy Son, satisfying Thee, exalting Thy name. Thy strength and Thy power are established in my heart; Thou art the living Disk; eternity is Thine emanation (or attribute)..."

- "He" (*i.e.*, Aten, the One God) "hath brought forth His honored Son, Ua-en-re (the Only One of the Sun) like His own form, never ceasing so to do. The Son of Re supporteth His beauties..."

- "Thou art in my heart. There is no other who knoweth Thee except Thy Son Nefer-kheperu-re Ua-en-re (Beautiful essence of the Sun, Only One of the Sun). Thou hast made him wise to understand Thy plans and Thy power..."

- "Every man who (standeth on his) feet since Thou didst lay the foundation of the earth, Thou hast raised up for Thy Son who came forth from Thy body, the King of the South and the North, Living in Truth, Lord of Crowns, Akhenaten, great in the duration of his life (and for) the Royal Wife, great in majesty, Lady of the Two Lands, Nefer-neferu-Aten Nefertiti, living (and) young for ever and ever."

These bold statements of his relationship to God cannot be understood in their proper sense unless one replaces them in their context, that is to say, in the whole system of ideas at the basis of the Religion of the Disk; especially unless one connects them with that hardly less bold assertion that the "Heat-and-light-within-the-Disk" and the Disk itself are one. This having been proved correct as a result of modern scientific speculations cannot be called "dogma." Yet, religiously speaking, it argues for the substantial *unity* of God and nature, visible and invisible; the existence of the same unchangeable thing—divine energy—at the bottom of all things visible and invisible, material and immaterial, which change everlastingly. In other words, for as much as one is able to infer from the hymns, Akhenaten's teaching seems to have been founded on an implicit if not explicit *pantheistic monism*.

What I wish to stress here is that, though he found nowhere around him anyone who possessed, like him, the knowledge of the unchangeable within the transient, he was aware that this direct, sensuous experience of oneness was the goal of created life. And he was aware that he himself, who had reached it, stood apart from the average man—as far apart from him, indeed, as he from the crowd of still less awakened sentient beings, if not further. He was a man—physically conceived and born as all men—and yet more than a man. He was, not merely in name but in fact, the Beautiful-essence-of-the-Sun, since he felt that essence, that indefinable energy, running through his nerves.

Akhenaten—the Joy of the Sun—became fully conscious of Itself within him; the Son of God, who was alone to know His Father. As the visible Disk and the invisible, intangible "heat and light," the energy within it, were one, so was he one with that same all-pervading radiant energy experienced within him. And he knew it. His nerves knew it. His body—a lump of matter finally tracing its origin to our parent star (like all matter on earth)—was aware of the power within its depth. God and created nature were one in him.

They were all the more one because he was, also, a man who lived to the full the happy natural life of all creatures. On the other hand, he could and he did live the natural life of the body and of the mind in perfect beauty and "in truth," only because he was a "realized soul," a perfect Individual—a Son of God.

THE RELIGION OF THE DISK

We can now try to sum up the essential features of the teaching which we have termed the "Religion of the Disk," and which Akhenaten regarded as the universal religion, and preached as such.

Based upon its founder's intuition of the equivalence of all forms of energy, of the identity of energy and of what appears to the senses as matter, and of his own substantial oneness with that same energy that is at the root of all existence, it represents, philosophically, a variety of pantheistic monism. It stands apart from other purely speculative systems, inasmuch as it was a cult as well as a philosophy. In it, the immanent soul of the Sun (and of the cosmos), "Heat-and-Light which is in the Disk"—radiant energy—was the object of a stately public worship comprising music and dancing and the singing of hymns, along with the ritual offering of food, drink, flowers, and incense. The only visible form, however, which the worshipper was allowed to consider, was the image of the Sun-disk with rays ending in hands, symbolizing the power radiating from the Sun down to the earth on which we live.

Akhenaten himself occupied a prominent place in the religion as the "Son of the Sun" or "Son of God"—that word designating not a man miraculously conceived, but the man who, while conceived and born like all creatures, had exhausted the highest possibilities of human nature by becoming directly conscious of the presence of the soul, or essence of the Sun within his nerves.

Queen Nefertiti, both as the wife who was a part of himself and as the true disciple who had wholeheartedly accepted him and his teaching, through love, was second only to him. And it is probable that, had the Religion of the Disk survived, it would have centered round these two figures—especially round its founder, looked upon as divine. Along with the intellectual worship of universal energy, it would have become the devotional cult of the perfect individual—the only one to deserve the name of "Son of the Sun." And any imaginable attempt to revive it would, if successful, result in the same; so inseparable is the teacher from his teaching.

The philosophical conclusions which can be drawn from the hymns have been confirmed by the general tendency of modern science to resolve matter into atoms, atoms into centers of power, and qualitatively different kinds of power into outward expressions of quantitative differences. They can therefore today be called positive knowledge, though they were, originally, the result of one man's apparently unaccountable intuition. It is to them that Petrie refers when he calls the Religion of the Disk a religion which could have been "invented to satisfy our modern scientific conceptions."

That other all-important idea of the unity of all life and brotherhood of all living creatures is based, at the same time, upon the general substantial pantheism of the Religion of the Disk; upon the fatherhood of our parent star, nourisher of all beings; and upon the response of even the meanest of living things to His beneficent heat and light.

Akhenaten's teaching can therefore in no way be compared to any of those faiths based upon the supernatural revelation of a personal God through miraculous happenings. It is connected with no miracles, save the everyday miracle of birth and growth, and that miracle of perfect beauty: the life of its founder. It is rational in the sense that its fundamentals express a human experience: that of universal oneness, and facts of this earth, such as the happy reaction of all creatures to the warmth of sunshine. But it draws its inspiration from the beauty of the Sun and of the natural world, and from the joy of life, more than from any precise theory of the universe.

At least to the extent to which we know of it, it puts forth no definite views about death and the destiny of the dead. Though a prayer, inscribed upon Akhenaten's coffin, suggests that he personally believed in the survival of consciousness in a much subtler state of corporeality, it seems as if the "problem of death" as well as the problem of suffering were deliberately left aside as insolvable when considered at our general human scale, and automatically solved for those who live "in truth."

Ethically, the religion was of the highest standard, implying absolute sincerity in thought, speech and action. And love, not for man alone, but for all living creatures considered as our brothers. This fact of its being by no means man-centered but "life-centered" places it, in my eyes, far above the later monotheisms that a few modern authors have endeavored to put in parallel with it. The god who has a "chosen people," and the god who is the father of all men but not of the rest of creatures, are equally alien to the all-pervading "Heat-and-Light within the Disk." And both are but puerile and barbaric tribal gods, compared with that truly universal Father-and-Mother of all life, whom the young Pharaoh adored.

To be truthful to the bitter end, with courage—with heroism if necessary—and to love all creatures and be kind to them is therefore the sacred duty of anyone who follows Akhenaten.

The condemnation of the revolting exploitation of animals and men—especially of that of the more helpless animals—which has kept on dishonoring mankind from before the dawn of history, is logically implied in the admission that we are all brothers in the Sun. We all are co-worshippers, at different levels of consciousness, of the one same principle of all life. Equally implied in it is the respect of trees and plants which are, also, in their own way, happy to thrive in the sunlight—a whole practical philosophy in which the God-conscious individual in tune with life as a whole is the centre, the purpose, the culmination of creation on earth. And this remains true, whether those who once called themselves Akhenaten's disciples lived up to their faith or whether they did not.

Yet, it is correct to say that the Religion of the Disk seems to have comprised no explicit commandments and prohibitions. It logically implied certain actions. It excluded certain others. It ordered nothing. It forbade nothing. It was not a device to keep the average man out of mischief, but a "teaching of life" addressed to those few whom their rational mind, their straightforward nature, and above all their sensitiveness to the beauty of the living sunny world predisposed to receive it. It was—it is—in one sense the only religion for all living creatures, and in another, a religion only for the elite of men.

Budge (1923: 96) tells us that "the Atenites adored and enjoyed the heat and light which their god poured upon them, and...sang and danced and praised his beneficence, and lived wholly in the present. And they worshipped the triad of life, beauty and color..." This is true in a sense, but there is more to say. That joy of life was not a superficial and sterile gaiety. It was a deep and elevating experience, an inspiration which led the worshipper as near the God-conscious King, true Son of the Sun, as the limitations of his individual nature permitted him to reach.

We have just now spoken of the practical implications of the teaching in the disciple's daily life. What we have yet to see of Akhenaten's unusual career illustrates the application of its principles by its very promoter to a problem of all times: the problem of war.

PART III:

TRUTH VERSUS SUCCESS

Fig. 10: Nefertiti kissing her daughter.

CHAPTER 9

WHAT WAS, AND WHAT MIGHT HAVE BEEN

In order to realize all the importance of what Akhenaten did—or abstained from doing—when the hard "necessities" of war were thrust upon him, one should first keep in mind the most exalted position which he occupied in the world of his days.

The Egyptian empire was, when he took it over by hereditary right, the greatest empire existing. It could certainly not be compared, either in extent or organization, with what the Roman Empire was one day to be. Far from it. But still, its frontiers stretched from the banks of the Upper Euphrates and the Amanus Mountains down to the Fourth Cataract of the Nile. The northern half of the empire was a conglomeration of innumerable small vassal states. Every Syrian or Canaanite town of little importance had its "king," who acknowledged himself as the "servant" of the faraway Pharaoh and paid tribute to him. The whole country was under the immediate supervision of a "governor of the northern countries" or "viceroy of the North."

Though there were various conflicts throughout the empire, none were as serious as those of the present-day Middle East—specifically, in Syria and Palestine. All that is known of the unrest there in Akhenaten's time can be gathered from a collection of some 350 clay tablets—the famous "Amarna Letters"—discovered in 1887 and 1891 on the site of the Pharaoh's ruined capital. These tablets, covered with cuneiform writing, represent what is left of the diplomatic correspondence of the young king and of his father. What was exactly the situation cannot be described with full accuracy of details; nor can one follow its evolution step by step, for the date of many of the letters is uncertain. Moreover, a great number of precious tablets have been completely destroyed through mishandling.

It can, however, be stated that "a great concerted anti-Egyptian movement," in which the Hittites were playing the local enemies of Egypt—and the "Habiru", the plundering tribes of the desert who joined the rebellion in Canaan—were attacking the loyal vassals of Egypt from the borders of the Euphrates down to the south of Palestine. They were fighting under the leadership of a growing number of chieftains of different races, if we judge by their names. The most prominent of these were Itakama, Abdashirta, and, especially after the death of the latter, his ambitious and unscrupulous son, Aziru.

Throughout the second half of Akenaten's reign, Aziru and the Hittites captured vast territories in the region—land that had long been until benign Egyptian rule. Pleas for aid poured in to the young King. But he took no action. He acted as though the land conquered by his fathers were not his. In other words, from the time he understood that a number of Syrian and Canaanite local dynasts did not want his rule, he ceased to consider himself as their overlord. He styled himself as such, it is true, in the letters that he sent even to such disloyal princes as Aziru. But that was because Aziru and all the others, however wildly anti-Egyptian, maintained a pretence of loyalty in their official correspondence with him. In fact, he never treated them or endeavored even to treat them as an overlord desiring to stress his rights would have done.

Akhenaten stood aloof from the war that was raging throughout his Asiatic dominions. But it was impossible for him to make anyone understand the motives of his apparently strange attitude. Nobody, not even those who professed to be his followers, could make out why his devotion to Aten, the one Sun, the one God, should clash with his imperial "duties." For they could not realize what the one Sun meant to him. They thought that he who had built in Syria a town destined to be, like Akhet-aten itself, a radiating centre of the new faith, would naturally do anything in his power to keep Syria under control. They could not realize that Akhenaten's impersonal God, the energy within the Disk, was not one to whom worshippers can be brought by a show of force.

They could not understand that knowledge, genuine religious experience, the vivid consciousness of universal unity, and universal order were at the basis of his cult, and that the hatred generated by conquest and kept alive in the conquered people by measures of violence, was utterly uncongenial to the creation of those conditions. The far-sighted logic of his attitude was alien to them. Even his beloved queen, Nefertiti, could probably not follow him. She just accepted what he did, out of personal devotion to him, without judging him, and kept her confidence in his mission until the end, because she loved him.

Still, he himself could not help seeing both sides of the conflict. He felt sympathy for his faithful vassals. He could not help feeling sympathy also for the "unfaithful" ones who were seeking to overthrow his rule, as his fathers had once overthrown the rule of the foreign Hyksos kings in Egypt. He could not help knowing that, at the root of all the trouble, lay the hatred that conquest always generates in a conquered people.

The one father—the Sun—had made all nations "distinct in speech and in the color of their skin," and He poured His life-giving rays over all of them. All were to live, happy and beautiful, and at peace. Conquest, the fruit of greed, was, like all forms of outrage, conceivable only to those who did not love the One Sun enough to love all His creatures impartially. And he, the son of the universal father, could not lend himself to the holding down of a restless conquered land. He could not prolong a state of things which ignorance, self-pride, and greed had once created. He was to have nothing to do with "imperial duties" that were in contradiction with the principle of impartial love. It was not for him, who lived in truth, to defend an order based upon falsehood.

PASSING OF A DIVINE SOUL

Akhenaten died prematurely. And it is possible that the grief he felt for those whom he appeared to be abandoning hastened his death. "With him," writes Breasted (1924: 127), passed away "such a spirit as the world had never seen before," and I would add: such as was never to reappear since. Eleven hundred years after him, India's great emperor Asoka was one day to renounce war in the name of the Buddha's message of universal love. But the question did not arise for him to retain or to lose for its sake the lands he had inherited from his fathers. He was allowed to die leaving his vast dominions prosperous and whole. Akhenaten seems to be the one king in history who, for the sake of a philosophy which logically excluded the support of any form of aggression, actually lost a great empire. The tragic circumstances which I have tried to recall and, on the other hand, the tremendous might and wealth that the young Pharaoh could have used to defend his imperial rights, make his sacrifice all the more remarkable.

And his message of love as a basis of international relations, in the place of the time-honored law of violence; his refusal to subscribe to conquest as a fait accompli of which the advantages to the conquering nation should be maintained anyhow, are all the more impressive precisely because they were proclaimed from a throne. They were proclaimed by the hereditary owner of the greatest empire of his days; by an absolute monarch, fully conscious of his immense wealth and power; by an emperor, whom his subjects were taught by tradition to look upon as divine—without their realizing how truly godlike he actually was.

AN ALTERNATE HISTORY

Let us suppose for a moment that, unlike himself, Akhenaten had yielded to the supplications of his few loyal vassals, and sent them timely help against the Amorite chieftains and their Hittite supporters. Let us even suppose that he had marched in person into Syria, with archers and chariots and all the awe-inspiring apparel of war, as any of his fathers would have done.

It is highly probable that in such a case the "sons of Abdashirta" would have been utterly defeated from the start, and the Syrian rebellion nipped in the bud. In spite of long years of peace, Egypt was still a first-rate military power. Moreover, the aid that was needed to re-assert her prestige was, in the beginning, extremely slight.

The youthful founder of the Religion of the Disk would have returned in triumph to his capital. The new City of the Horizon of Aten would have gazed upon one of those impressive displays of warrior-like pomp such as Thebes had witnessed in former days. And the bitterness and resentment caused by the erasure of the name of Amun from every stone and by the king's other decrees, and by his whole struggle against the national gods, would have been forgotten in a cry of victory. And Egypt would probably have accepted the rational worship of Aten, the one and only God, without further murmurs.

Not that the people or even the nobles would have understood it, or felt its beauty, any better than they actually did. But they would have accepted it, as the expression of the sweet will of a popular king. The fact that, in spite of his revolutionary decrees, not a single rising is reported against his government in Egypt during all his reign, proves that Akhenaten was popular enough among his subjects. The only thing the Egyptians could not bring themselves to do for his sake was to renounce their traditional objects of worship in favor of a higher one. The only force that could have led them to forsake even their beloved gods, at the command of him whom they still regarded as a god incarnate, was the prestige of victory added to that of royalty.

The orders of a monarch who has brought an empire to ruin, even if he be of divine descent, do not indeed carry the same weight as those of a triumphant king. There is, in armed success, a magic that commands respect, whatever be the personal views of the lucky warrior. One has seen in modern times, nay, in our own days, men inferior by far to Akhenaten in genius and in character succeed in stamping their will upon a reluctant nation, just because they had, first, led that nation to victory upon the battlefield. And I believe that nothing would have so reconciled the unwilling Egyptians to the new order installed by their inspired ruler as the knowledge that he had saved them and their empire from imminent danger.

The more I think of the situation created in Egypt by Akhenaten's zeal for truth, the more I am convinced that brilliant military achievements beyond the Sinai Desert were the one and only means for him to secure the lasting success of his reforms at home.

A New Life

The enduring success of Akhenaten's religion in Egypt would have meant more than a change of cult. It would have meant new standards in art and in behavior; sincerity of thought, freedom of expression, a critical, disinterested, truth-loving attitude in all walks of life. In one word, a new life.

What is left of the Amarna sculpture and painting shows us the beginning of an amazing return to personal inspiration in art, to naturalness, to freedom. With the failure of the Religion of the Disk, the artistic movement linked with it was stifled to death at its very outset. What it would have been, had it lived, is difficult to say. But one may imagine, from its earliest creations, that it would have anticipated ideals of beauty that we now call "modern," putting far greater stress upon expression than upon lines, and striving to reveal the inner nature of things, rather than their exact or embellished physical likeness.

We can somewhat picture to ourselves the subsequent development of Egypt had her art, henceforth, been inspired by the Amarna standards. Imagine the situation, had her religion remained that which Akhenaten preached; had there appeared, from time to time, true disciples of the one-who-lived-in-truth, who would have modeled their lives upon his; had her whole civilization retained the double mark of rationalism and of universal kindness and the essentially aesthetic outlook on life that characterized her only truly divine king. Then, even making the indispensable allowances for human wickedness and stupidity, the country, merely by seeking to walk in the trail of such a man as Akhenaten, would have put itself far ahead of all the neighboring nations. It would have been a modern country in the midst of the ancient world—but a modern country retaining all that was lovely in ancient life. It would have been a nation without the horrors that our world of today has brought into existence by the import of greater technical efficiency combined with less reason, less inspiration, and less love.

A New Society

But Egypt was not alone concerned. She occupied in the world, then, the position of a great power. Her gods, like those of all leading nations, were worshipped beyond her boundaries. It is probable that the cult of Aten had not reached, in Akhenaten's days, the limits of the Egyptian dominions. But there is little doubt that, had it once been able to establish itself firmly in the Nile Valley, the Religion of the Disk would have spread throughout the empire and even to allied countries—to all lands where the power of the Pharaoh was dreaded and his name held in reverence. From Napata to Carchemish, over a stretch of 20 degrees of latitude, the name of Aten, the God above all gods, would have become familiar to people of the most various races.

How little those myriads of men would have grasped of the true spirit of Akhenaten's teaching is useless to say. But even a partial and altogether outward knowledge of it would have sufficed to impress upon them the idea of the excellence of a natural worship, of cosmic significance, over their thousand and one man-made cults of local scope. It would have sufficed, also, to inspire all those who were susceptible of some refinement with the feeling of the beauty of the world and of the unity of all life.

And possibly Egypt and the adjoining countries would have remained, to this day, faithful to the cult of the one God manifested in the Sun. It seems indeed doubtful whether any later monotheistic creed would have found adherents among thinking people already acquainted for centuries with Akhenaten's teaching.

A NEW CIVILIZATION

The worship of Aten, had it remained the state-religion of Egypt—of a victorious Egypt, mistress of her empire—would have undoubtedly influenced the whole evolution of Western thought and culture.

Even in her decline, after every sort of originality had been killed in her priest-ridden people, Egypt still exerted a lasting influence upon Greece. What would that influence have been, had Egypt remained powerful a few centuries longer, and had the simple and rational Sun-worship preached by Akhenaten continued to hold sway over her, instead of the more and more formal, the more and more fossilized cult of her primitive gods? A glance at these possibilities will be enough to show what Akhenaten could perhaps have done, had he but consented to utter a word in favor of war.

The whole of the young king's teaching is characterized by an unusual *rationality*, allied to an overwhelming sense of *beauty*. It is probable that, in the days of its founder—200 years before the Trojan War—no account of it reached the shores of Greece. And had, by chance, some exiled Egyptian ever carried it there, we do not know what impression it would have left upon the people of Tiryns and Mycenae. But had the scientific-minded leaders of Grecian thought come in contact with the teaching some centuries later, at the time Greece was ready to enter the maturity of her classical age, then, I believe, the history of Western civilization would have been different.

The skeptical Athenian mind, while continuing to pay a customary allegiance to "the gods of the city," would have welcomed that rational creed that put stress upon nothing which is outside the reach of man's experience—one that related no incredible deeds, no childish fables. The few who aspired to something more than intellectual certitude would have recognized the truth in a teaching that implied the oneness and sacredness of life. And the Greeks at large would have felt in Akhenaten's worship a thing of beauty, unsurpassed even in their own land of light and harmony.

And slowly the time would have come for a great change in the consciousness of the ancient world. The time when, tired of conflicting philosophies as well as of rites and mysteries of which they had forgotten the sense, the Greeks would have begun to aspire to something unknown which they could neither define nor invent. The time when, in a word, the need of a broader and kinder outlook even than that of the best Athenians would have begun to be felt throughout the Hellenized world. Then, instead of turning her eyes to any new creed, perhaps Greece would have simply drifted from the worship of her many gods to that of the only one revealed to men and to all creatures through the flaming Disk of the Sun. And without sacrificing anything of her passionate love of life and visible beauty, without also forcing herself to accept any dogmas "beyond reason" or "above reason," perhaps she would have made the 1,400-year-old Religion of the Disk the creed of her people for all times to come.

There would have been no conflict between an "old" and a "new" order. Rather, merely a gradual absorption of the popular religions of Greece and Rome into the decorous simplicity of a more rational, more spiritual, and more ancient one, already held in regard by the elite of the Greek-speaking East.

And slowly but steadily, along with the culture and learning of the Mediterranean, the antique worship of Aten would have spread over barbaric Europe, replacing the popular cults of the North after those of Asia Minor, Greece, and Italy. On the borders of the Danube and of the Rhine, on the misty shores of the Baltic and of the North Sea, temples containing no image but the Sun Disk with rays ending in hands would have been erected in honor of the one God—cosmic energy.

And one day, the Spanish caravelles would have carried the lofty symbol across the Atlantic, and the Religion of the Disk would have become the religion of the West.

What Might Have Been

Would the West, then, have been any better than it is? Perhaps not. Even with all the overwhelming loveliness of his living personality Akhenaten could not, in his days, improve human nature. It is doubtful whether his surviving teaching—somewhat distorted, as might be expected, by clumsy interpreters—would have been able to accomplish that miracle.

Most probably the same passions would have disturbed the peace of the world. But they would not have been fanned by religious fanaticism, and that alone would have made an enormous difference. The opposition of the different national polytheisms to the universal worship of such a God as the Sun would never, it seems, have taken the form of such a ferocious conflict as witnessed in the first centuries of the Christian era between the same old national cults and the gospel preached by Paul of Tarsus.

The adoration of light is a thing so natural and universal that it would have been easy to convince both philosophers and barbarians of its excellence. The Emperor Julian would have been the first one to encourage a creed more rational and no less aesthetic than those of his Greek masters. And the Western world would never have known such atrocities as the ghastly murder of Hypatia or the mass-massacre of the Saxons. There would have not been any equivalent of the Crusades, or of the wars of the Arabs for the conversion of infidels, or of the Holy Inquisition. Greed and cruelty would have remained, but in order to gratify such base passions it would hardly have been possible to exploit a religion free from puerile hopes no less than from superstitious fears.

No doubt, one day, the newly-discovered hemisphere would have been overrun by the same merciless adventurers in search of gold. The same battles would have raged in Mexico, in Guatemala, and in Peru, around the last bastions of American independence. But they would have been battles frankly fought for the possession of earthly goods, not for the triumph of the faith, not for the salvation of souls, not "for the greatest glory of God." The interview of Pizarro and Atahualpa would have been different. In the God of the Inca, "Who lives for ever in the sky," the Spanish conqueror would have recognized his own God. And both he and the Peruvian king would have felt that, whatever be their behavior towards each other, they had in common something vital. The fortunate people of the New World would have learned to link what was the best in their own traditions with a purer and more rational worship of the Sun.

And the world today would have been, if not more peaceful, at least better prepared to realize its fundamental unity within everlasting diversity. On the whole, it would have been, it seems, a better world.

A DREAM UNFULFILLED

This retrospective vision of centuries of would-be history is staggering. Yet I believe it is not the projection of a pure fancy. That gigantic dream of ours was, 3,300 years ago, a living possibility. That more rational, more harmonized, more beautiful world, united under the symbol of the Sun-disk with rays ending in hands, could well have become the reality of today—had then the one man with a clear vision of the truth used his wealth and power to keep the empire of his fathers, and to force his will upon his people.

That better world was the possible reward of a short and successful punitive expedition against a handful of agitators. Less than that: it was the reward of an order to Horemheb, or to any other of his generals, to march into Syria, without the king even taking the trouble of going there himself. It was the remote consequence of *a single word.*

But, for the reasons we have seen, that word was never uttered.

While the distressed letters from his loyal vassals came pouring in from Syria, Akhenaten quietly continued to greet the rising and setting Sun as though nothing else counted. He read the pathetic messages one after the other—in what spirit and with what reactions, he alone knew. And he spoke not. He refused to set in motion the long series of events that would have given him uncontested spiritual domination over the Western world.

Fig. 11: Akhenaten, Nefertiti, and children (detail of Fig. 1).

CHAPTER 10

THE PRICE OF PERFECTION

There can be little doubt that, as time passed on, Akhenaten became more and more aware of the difficulty of the task he had chosen. The strongly organized opposition of the priests that he never succeeded in breaking taught him that there was nothing to expect from persuasion. And it seems impossible for him not to have understood, with his keen intelligence, that the only way to lasting religious domination left to him was that of immediate violence.

The common people of Egypt—like the common people of all countries in all times—were to be led like a flock of sheep. They would listen to the priests as long as there were priests to be listened to. Akhenaten knew it. The one and only way to put an end to the influence of Amun's servants upon the ignorant folk was to have them exterminated. But, as we have already seen, the king did nothing of the kind. He was content to confiscate the scandalous wealth of the priests; and he let their persons go uninjured. As for the educated and well-to-do Egyptians, who knew what the greatness of Egypt and her empire meant to them in riches and prestige, their permanent adherence to the new teaching depended largely upon its value as a national creed. There are reasons to believe that even such a man as Merira, the High-priest of Aten, on whom the king had founded great hopes, failed to stand by his master when he realized that the Religion of the Disk was costing Egypt her empire. Akhenaten knew that also.

And a time must have come when he beheld, with desperate lucidity, the choice set before him: either to wage war upon Aziru and his allies, to re-assert the right of Egypt to be the leading nation, and to win for himself, in return, the triumph of the cult of Aten; *or else*, to continue following the path he had taken, and to end in disaster, in anathema, and finally in oblivion.

GLORY AT HAND

The religious success that the Pharaoh could contemplate as the reward of a compromise would surely seem small to us, compared with that staggering domination of more than half the globe. It was, however, no less impressing to him who considered its possibility. But knowing, as he certainly did, what a force Egypt represented in the midst of the surrounding nations, he must have clearly realized that, if successful at home, his religion would have spread even to the farthermost regions that he could imagine. And the triumph which he thus anticipated must have appeared to him as universal. It was the triumph of reason, the triumph of truth; the beginning of a kindlier and more beautiful world. It was the fulfillment of his lifelong struggle, which had so far seemed fruitless; the magnificent reward that would outweigh for all times to come the bitterness of the few years in which he had stood alone, misunderstood or hated. It was *his* triumph.

If we recall the foundation of Akhet-aten, it cannot but strike us that, once at least in his short career, Akhenaten had desired success. An inscription, carved out on one of the boundary-stones of the city, and relating to the king's burial, reflects his joyous hopes. "And there shall be made for me a sepulcher in the Eastern hills," runs the writing. "My burial shall be made there in the multitude of jubilees that Aten, my Father, hath ordained for me, and the burial of the queen shall be made there in that multitude of years." Obviously, he then visualized the life that spread before him, as a long succession of radiant years in which the truth that he felt so deeply would triumph through him. He had the self-confidence of youth, the unhesitating optimism of intense desire allied to boundless power. It was his will to change the face of things. He had no doubt that he would do so. And he was too human not to feel the thrill of coming glory.

And now, that glory was at hand, if he so wished. The words inscribed upon stone at his command, ten years before, could still be true. At the cost of a slight compromise—so slight that no one would ever find it out—his name, otherwise destined to be cursed and to perish, could still be honored "in a multitude of jubilees," not during his lifetime, but during the countless centuries the world had yet to live. If he so wished, the future of mankind could still be brightened by his light, and marked with his sign.

The few sincere disciples he still retained at court were impatient to hear him utter the word that implied compromise and success. They longed to hear him give the order to save the empire.

Why then did Akhenaten remain silent?

A Commitment to Peace

As I have said, there seems to have been an innate repulsion for bloodshed. The idea of war, like that of persecution, was repugnant to his sensitive nature. The brutalities inherent to any punitive expedition seemed to him too irredeemably ugly even to be tolerated as a necessary evil.

But it would not be doing full justice to his memory to look upon the king of Egypt as the Bronze Age equivalent of our modern pacifists. Akhenaten was neither a Christian nor a democrat. His religion was, before all, an *aesthetic* one. His morality sprang from his all-pervading sense of beauty. His conscientious objection to war was not the product of any narrow, uncritical love confined to the human species, but the logical consequence of his serene understanding of universal harmony. He desired to see the behavior of intelligent beings reflect, as far as possible, the beautiful inner order of the cosmos. And he hated all forms of cruelty—the worst conceivable expressions of moral ugliness.

I think it would be a mistake to suppose that the sole cause of his inaction in the Syrian affair was Akhenaten's belief in a creed condemning war indiscriminately. Had it been so, such a consistent man as he was would never have allowed Pakhura to go north with his soldiers. Nor would he, in the only letter of his which we possess, have spoken as a monarch instead of speaking as a preacher. It is much more probable that Akhenaten's attitude to war was a *negative* one; an attitude of non-interest, rather than one of systematic opposition.

The founder of the Religion of the Disk seems to have seen both sides of the problem of violence. All atrocities disgusted him, whatever were the "higher motives" that urged men to commit them. And he was aware that war leads nowhere in the long run. He saw things, not from a national point of view, not even from a human point of view, but from that of cosmic reality. And therefore it mattered little to him whether Egypt had an empire or not.

He knew that, with all the power inherited from generations of king-gods, he could do nothing to stop the fighting going on within his realm. The only reasonable course left to him was indeed to keep himself aloof from it, serene and alone as he had always been. And that is precisely what he did.

THE PRICE OF SILENCE

But what astonishes the modern man perhaps more than Akhenaten's total absence of "imperialism" is his apparent indifference to the success of his religion. If he so loved his faithful servant, Ribaddi, as to allow troops to be sent to his rescue, then how did he not consider it worthwhile dispatching more substantial help to all his loyal vassals and, if necessary, marching into Syria himself—if not to defend the interests of Egypt, at least to secure the adherence of Egypt to his teaching?

The only answer is that he probably cared less for the success of his teaching than for its purity. And he knew that success and purity seldom go together. He was not over-impressed by numbers, as lesser men often are. He knew their futility in the long run. What he wanted was that those who would "hearken to his teaching" should mould their lives upon it—"live in truth," as he did. And experience had made him aware that very few were able to do so.

When, followed by more than 80,000 people, he had left Thebes and laid the foundations of his new capital, he may have for a time rejoiced at the idea of his teaching spreading to the limits of his dominions and beyond. If not, one could hardly explain why he took the trouble of founding at least two other centers of rational Sun-worship, one at each end of his vast empire. But at the time the Syrian rebellion had reached its climax, Akhenaten had probably become conscious of the uselessness of all efforts to make his religion a success among men, if it was to remain as beautiful and as rational as he had conceived it. He knew that, in spite of all the care he had taken to make it accessible to the most intelligent of his courtiers, he had no true disciple, except perhaps his loving consort.

In that case, what was the value of worldly success? Of name? Of fame? Even of the recognized spiritual leadership of half the globe or more? It was as nothing.

Akhenaten knew that by keeping his empire whole he could soon propagate his religion as far as the remotest countries he could think of. But he could also foresee that the cult that would perhaps, one day, unite those distant lands in the glorification of his name would no longer be the religion of life in truth. No. It would perhaps be something better than what men had called "religion" until then. It would perhaps even be something better than what the majority of mankind would ever accept, in the future, as a guide to a higher life. But it would never be that glorious worship he had dreamt of in his days of youthful hopes—the true Religion of the Disk.

It was certainly no use silencing his personal disgust for bloodshed, and compromising with his principles, merely to magnify, in space and time, the disappointing triumph he had already experienced during his short career. If the elite of Egypt had not really accepted his teaching, what would the empire at large and the nations beyond the empire make of it? What would most men of the future ages make of it, when in their hearts they probably would not feel its truth; when they would not understand it, not love it, not want it? Akhenaten saw clearly that his religious leadership, when extended to millions, would amount to nothing but the gradual re-installment of superstition, under the cover of his name—the degradation of his dearest dreams. And he refused to give his sanction to it.

And one may safely believe that, even if he could have imagined the possibility of the Religion of the Disk becoming one day the official faith of far-away lands, at the cost of a compromise that could seem trifling, he still would not have stirred his little finger to promote such a success. The disappointment of triumph on a small scale and for a few brief years was enough.

IMMORTAL PERFECTION

From the moment Akhenaten refused to bend his uncompromising logic to the exigencies of ordinary colonial policy, the fate of his beautiful Sun-worship was sealed. No later compromise could henceforth be introduced, by subtle casuistry, to make it "fit in" with the accepted conceptions of national grandeur, or with the accepted opinion that any course of action is good which leads to the attainment of a "higher goal." The founder of the Religion of the Disk had once and for all barred the possibility of such convenient adjustments, by the bold example of his own solution of the problem of religion and state. He had made it clear that, to him, there was no higher goal than that of "life in truth," which is another word for individual perfection.

There are portraits of him which show us a thin, sickly face, with deep wrinkles each side of the mouth, and bones jutting out: the face of a young man worn out by sorrow and possibly also by some wasting disease. These portraits bear little resemblance to those of his early youth, except for the unbending determination that can be read in the king's features. Given every allowance for the exaggerations and distortions that seem to have been part of the "style" of several artists of the court, there can be no doubt that they reveal to us something of the appearance of their royal model at some stage of his life, probably at the last stage. If so, they help us to visualize Akhenaten's heroic stand to the bitter end.

He was still very young—at an age when most great men have not yet begun to do the work for which they are born. But he was a physical wreck, and conscious that his end was drawing nigh. He had married his eldest daughter, the heiress to the kingdom, aged twelve, to a young man of royal blood, Smenkhkare, who was devoted to him and to his cause. Out of reverence and gratitude, Smenkhkare had taken, in official documents, the title of "beloved of Akhenaten."

But the king knew that, with all his good intentions, that prince would not for long be able to postpone the fierce reaction that was to break out. He knew that the dispossessed priests of Amun were gathering more and more strength as news of national disaster rapidly spread throughout Egypt. He knew that, in the very near future, the Religion of the Disk would be swept out of the land, perhaps never to be revived again anywhere in any age. He knew that the incommunicable truth he had cherished all his life would never again be made to inspire the conduct of a State. And he had no grounds to imagine that the scientific principles that underlay his teaching would receive, in 3,300 years to come, an illuminating demonstration, and become the basis of what is to us modern science. To him it must have seemed as if his whole mission had been a complete failure.

Yet he knew that his teaching was true, and that truth cannot be destroyed. His name might be forgotten, but the fundamentals of the religion of order and love which he had discovered within the Sun and within himself would endure forever. Sooner or later, the human mind would have to rediscover them. And if one day some accident should bring his teaching to light again, then, at least, it would be unmarred by any practical compromise. And the most enlightened and the best of men would be able to love it without reservation. One day, perhaps, in many, many years to come, a few among the wise, truthful, and strong would revere him precisely for his refusal to tamper with truth. The unknown devotion of one of those few would be enough to outweigh the loss of an empire, the failure of a life of struggle, and millennia of oblivion.

And even if those one or two obscure disciples were never to be born; if the teaching for the sake of which he had lost everything were never to bear fruit, even in the heart of a single man; if the world to come would always listen to the priests of its national gods and never to him, the priest of the universal Sun; if he, Akhenaten, were to remain forever a useless dreamer—then, what of it all?

The Sun would nevertheless continue to follow, day after day, its glorious course, and it would still be true that "breath of life is to see His beams." Light and heat, and the spark that produces life, would still be the manifestations of the one energy—the soul of the Sun. Rhythm would still remain the principle of the universe, whether man cared to know it or not. Akhenaten's teaching would still be true, and his life a thing of beauty forever. Had the king of Egypt, in a moment of weakness, sacrificed the logic of his being to the lure of success, the future of mankind would perhaps have been, as we have seen, less gloomy, on the whole, than it actually was. But Akhenaten's personal history—an indestructible fact in the infinity of time, whether remembered or not—would not have been that flash of beauty which it is. The world would have been poorer of one perfect Individual.

And that was enough to make any loss worthwhile. His contemporary Egyptians seem to have preferred his empire to himself. But I prefer him to all the empires of the earth. And provided they be sufficiently sensitive to the real value of humanity, the men of ages to come will feel as I do.

END OF AN ERA

Akhenaten died in his 29th year, which was the 17th year of his reign. We know nothing of his last days or of the circumstances of his death. We can only try to imagine them. We can think of him gradually thrusting aside the burden of government after the elevation of Smenkhkare to the rank of co-regent, and living in retirement in his summer-house, in the midst of the beautiful gardens that lay to the south of his city. From his sickbed, Akhenaten gazed at the deep blue sky—light and peace—and his heart was happy. I like to imagine his dying in beauty, as he had lived, in a last effort to lift his enfeebled hands in praise to the rising Sun.

His lofty religion was swept out of Egypt. After the ephemeral reign of Smenkhkare, the priests of Amun regained great power. Akhenaten's city was pulled down stone by stone, and ruined so completely that men forgot where it had once stood. His body, torn from the tomb in the Eastern hills where he had desired to rest, was reburied in the Valley of the Tombs of the Kings, near Thebes. His name was effaced from the monuments, from his own coffin—even from the ribbons of gold foil that encircled his mummy, so that his soul might wander forever in hunger and agony.

In the pride of their recent triumph, the priests composed the exultant hymn of hate, addressed to the triumphant god Amun, and now preserved upon an ostracon in the British Museum:

> Thou findest him who transgresses against thee;
> Woe to him who assails thee!
> Thy city endures,
> but he who assailed thee falls.
> The sun of him who knows thee not goes down, O Amun!
> But as for him who knows thee, he shines.
> The abode of him who assailed thee is in darkness;
> but the rest of the earth is in light.
> Whoever puts thee in his heart, O Amun,
> Lo, his sun dawns.

And the world was once more, apparently at least, as though Akhenaten had never been born.

Fig. 12: Akhenaten and family make an offering to the Aten.

CHAPTER 11

AKHENATEN AND THE WORLD OF TODAY

Whatever one may think of Akhenaten's teaching, one has to concede at least three points concerning it.

First, the Religion of the Disk was a universal religion, as opposed to the former local or national religions of the ancient world. The supreme reality round which it centered—call it the soul of the Sun, the energy within the Disk, or give it any other name—was not only something worthy of the adoration of all men, but also something actually worshipped by all creatures. And all creatures, brought forth and sustained by the one source of life—the Sun—were one in Him. Never in the world west of India had the idea of universal divinity been so emphatically stressed, and the brotherhood of all living beings more deeply felt. And never were those truths to be stressed again more boldly in the future.

Second, it was a rational and natural religion—not a dogmatic one. It was neither a creed nor a code of human laws. It did not pretend to reveal the unknowable, or to regulate in details the behavior of man, or to offer means to escape the visible world and its links. It simply invited us to draw our religious inspiration from the beauty of things as they are: to worship life, in feeling and in deed; or, to put it as Nietzsche has done, to "remain true to the earth."[1] Based as it was, not upon any mythology but upon a broad intuition of scientific truth, its appeal would have increased with the progress of accurate knowledge—instead of decreasing, like that of many a better-known religion.

Finally, it was, from the very start, a teaching that exalted the individual perfection (*"living in truth"*) as the supreme goal, and at the same time a state-religion. Not only the religion *of* a State, but a religion *for* the State—for any and every State—no less than for the individual. It was a teaching in which the same idea of "truth" that was to inspire personal behavior through and through. It was also to determine the attitude of a monarch towards the friends and foes of his realm, to guide his decisions regarding peace and war; in one word, to dominate international relations. It implied, not the separation of private and public life, but their identity—their subjection to the same rational and aesthetic principles.

---

[1] *Thus Spoke Zarathustra*, Prologue (sec. 3).

Such was the message of Akhenaten, the only great religious teacher who was at the same time a king. He was perhaps the only undoubtedly historic originator of a religion on earth, who, being a king, did not renounce kingship but tried to tackle the problems of State—particularly the problem of war—in the light of religious truth.

The 17 years of Akhenaten's personal rule were but a minute in history. But that minute marks a level of perfection hardly ever approached in subsequent years.

When, under the pressure of his masters, the priests of Amun, Tutankhaten (renamed Tutankhamen), signed the decree reinstalling the national gods of Egypt in their former glory, he opened an era of intellectual conflict and moral unrest which has not yet today come to an end. Before Akhenaten, the world had worshipped national gods, and had been satisfied. After him, it continued to worship national gods, but was no longer fully content with them. For a minute, a new light had shone. Great truths—the universality of the supreme essence; the oneness of all life; the unity of religious and rational thought—had been proclaimed in words, in song, and in deeds, by one of those men who appear once in history. The man had been cursed, and it was henceforth a crime even to utter his name.

He was soon forgotten. But there was no way to suppress the fact that he had come. The old order of blissful ignorance was gone forever. Against its will, the world dimly remembered the light that the priests had sought to put out. And age after age, inspired men of various lands set out in search of the lost treasure. Some caught a glimpse of it, but none were able to regain it in its integrity. The Western world is still seeking it—in vain.

HISTORY REEXAMINED

To make my thought clear to all, let me briefly recap the evolution of the West from the overthrow of Akhenaten's work to the present day. With the earliest *physiologoi* of Ionia—800 years after Akhenaten—rational thought made its second appearance in the West. And this time it did not wither away after the death of one man, but found its mouthpieces in many. Generations of thinkers whose ambition was intellectual knowledge succeeded one another. Among them were such men as Pythagoras and Plato, who united the light of mystic insight to the clear knowledge of mathematics, and who transcended the narrow religious conceptions of their times.

But the Greek world could never transcend them. Socrates died "for not believing in the gods in whom the city believed," though there had been no more faithful citizen than he. Those gods were jealous and vengeful in their way. They would have been outdated and harmless had men accepted, a thousand years before, the worship of the one essence of all things, with all it implied. But they had not; and the conflict between the better individuals and the religion of the State had begun.

Rational thought was left to thrive; but not so the broad religious outlook that was linked with it. Theoretically, any universal God was acceptable. But the conception of something to be loved more than the state and worshipped before the national gods was alien to Greece, to Rome, and in general to all the city-minded people of the Mediterranean. Seen from our modern angle of vision, there was a strange disparity between the high intellectual standard of the Hellenes of classical times and their all-too-human local gods, in no way different from those of the other nations of the Near East.

Christianity was the next great wave in the history of Western conscious-ness. And one can hardly conceive a sharper contrast than that which exists between the clear Hellenic genius and the spirit of the creed destined to overrun Hellas, Europe, and finally America. It was originally—as preached by Paul of Tarsus—an irrational and unaesthetic creed, fed on miracles, bent on asceticism, strongly stressing the power of evil, ashamed of the body and afraid of life.

But its God was a universal God, and a God of love. Not as universal as might have been expected from a supreme being proposed to the adoration of a rationally-trained people; nor as impartially loving as a follower of the long-forgotten Religion of the Disk would have imagined his God to be. It was a God who, in fact, never shook off entirely some of the crude attributes which he possessed when worshipped by the Jews as their tribal deity. It was a God who gave man alone an immortal soul, infinitely precious in his eyes, for he loved man in the same childishly partial way as old Jehovah loved the Jewish nation. It was a *democratic* God who hated the well-to-do, the high-born, and also those who put their confidence in human intellect instead of submitting to the authority of his Gospel; who hid his truth "from the wise and the learned, but revealed it to the children" (Matt 11:25).

Christianity had the practical advantage of appealing both to the intellec-tually uncritical, to the emotionally unbalanced, and to the socially oppressed or neglected—that is to say, to the majority of mankind. That advantage, com-bined with the genuine appeal of a gospel of love and with the imperial patronage of Constantine, determined its final triumph. From the shores of the Eastern Mediterranean, it slowly but steadily spread to the whole of Europe and to all lands that European civilization has conquered.

But the Western world could not definitely forget centuries of rational thought. Nor could it renounce forever that avowed ideal of visible beauty, of strength, of cleanliness that had been connected with the various religions of the ancients. As far as was possible, it soon re-installed Greek metaphysics and polytheism under a new form in the very midst of Christianity. And later on, the Greek love of song and pleasure, and the deification of the human body, in the plastic arts as well as in life, prevailed in the spiritual capital of Christendom and throughout most Christian countries. The Western man gradually came to realize what an amount of inconsistency there was in that mixture of Hellenic and Hebrew thought which composed his traditional religion. He then grew increasingly skeptical, and Christianity remained for him little more than a poetic but obsolete mythology. The tardy reaction of the bold critical spirit of classical Hellas against Judeo-scholastic authority had come. And modern rationalism had made its way.

CHRISTIANITY VERSUS RATIONALISM

Now, if we turn to the latter reaction against the shortcomings of Christianity—namely, rationalism—we find that it has left the people who have matured under its influence in a state of moral unrest.

Modern rationalism may have, to some extent, taught the present-day Westerner to think in terms of cosmic realities. *But it has not yet taught him to feel in terms of cosmic values.* It has denounced Christian metaphysics as obsolete. But it still clings to the no less obsolete man-centered conception of right and wrong. It no longer maintains that man alone has an immortal soul, and it has forsaken the naïve idea that the world and all it contains was purposely created for man.

But it seems to see no harm in man's exploiting, destroying, or even torturing for his own ends the beautiful innocent creatures, animals and plants, nourished by the same sunshine as himself in the womb of the same mother Earth. For all practical purposes, it seems to consider them no more worthy of attention than if they were, indeed, created for him—by that very God of the Bible.

There are, of course, free-thinkers who have personally gone beyond the limits of Christian love and embraced all life in their sympathy. But these individual cases cannot blind us to the fact that neither of the two great movements that sprang up to supersede Christianity, has actually emphasized that fundamental truth of the unity of all life which the Christian Scriptures had omitted to express. There are, no doubt, remarkable Christians—for instance, Saint Francis of Assisi—who have grasped that truth and lived up to it. Still, in the omission of the Gospel to put the slightest stress upon it, lies the main weakness of Christianity compared with the lost Religion of the Disk. The only two large-scale attempts ever made west of India to restore to men the consciousness of that all-important truth were Pythagorism in antiquity, and nowadays Theosophy. The interest shown for the latter by many of our educated contemporaries points out how much ordinary rationalism is insufficient to meet the moral needs of the most sensitive among us.

THE CULT OF REASON

Modern rationalism has completely dissociated the idea of positive knowledge—of science—from that of worship. Not that a man of science cannot be, at the same time, a man of faith, but he considers the two domains as separate from each other. Their objects, he thinks, cannot be interchanged any more than their aims. One does not know God as one knows the data of sensuous experience or the logical conclusions of an induction. And however much one may admire the supremely beautiful picture of visible reality that modern science gives us, one cannot worship the objects of scientific investigation.

And the tragedy is that, once a rational picture of the world has imposed itself upon our mind, the usual objects of faith appear more and more as poetic fictions, as hidden allegories, or as deified moral entities. We do not want to do away with them altogether; yet we cannot help regretting the absence, in them, of that character of intellectual certitude that makes us cling so strongly to science. We feel more and more that moral certitude is not enough to justify our wholehearted adoration of any supreme principle. In other words, we feel that religion without a solid scientific background is insufficient.

On the other hand, there are moments when we regret the lost capacity of enjoying the blessings of faith with the simplicity of a child. We wonder, at times, if the men who built the Gothic cathedrals were not, after all, happier and better men than our contemporaries; if the tremendous inspiration they drew from childish legends was not worth all our barren "rational" beliefs. We would like to experience, in the exaltation of the "realities" which we value, the same religious fervor which they used to feel in the worship of a God who was perhaps an illusion.

But that seems impossible. Men have tried it and failed. The cult of the Goddess Reason put forward by the dreamers of the French Revolution, and the cult of Humanity, which Auguste Comte wished to popularize, could never make the Western man forget the long-loved sweetness of his Christian festivals, interwoven with all the associations of childhood. How could one even think of replacing the tradition of Christmas and Easter by such dry stuff as that? Science, without the advantages of religion, is no more able to satisfy us than religion without a basis of scientific certitude. Prominent as some of them may be, the men who nowadays remain content with rationalism are already out of date. The 20th century is growing more and more aware of its craving for some all-embracing truth, intellectual and spiritual, in the light of which the revelations of experience and faith, the dictates of science and religion, would find their place as partial aspects of a harmoniously organic whole.

A RELIGION FOR OUR TIME

Let us now look back to Akhenaten's teaching, of which I have recalled the main features at the beginning of this chapter. The more we examine it, in the light of 3,300 years of history, the more we are convinced that it is the perfect religion—toward which the Western world is still groping without being able to re-imagine it.

It has the advantage of being simple and complete. It is perhaps indeed the simplest among the lofty teachings of the whole world. It is a framework, suggesting an attitude towards the possible problems of individual and public life, rather than a system offering solutions of those problems once and for all. It is not only free from all mythology, from affirmations of any sort about things that are not known for certain, but it has hardly any tenets. To call it a creed is nearly a misuse of the word. It comprises no "theory," even about the world of facts. It is not a doctrine concerning science—which could grow out of date. Yet, it is based upon a bold scientific intuition which has not only been proved correct, but is broad enough to contain and sum up, after so many centuries, the essential of man's positive knowledge of the universe, and which thus confers upon the whole of it the permanent strength of intellectual certitude. It has no catalogue of imperatives, and makes no mention of right and wrong. Yet, the fervent love expressed in Akhenaten's hymns implies the noblest behavior towards all living things—even towards one's enemies—and historic events have shown that the implication was not an empty one.

Finally, the fact that the promoter of the teaching was the ruler of a first-rate military power, with foreign possessions and vassal states, and that he put the spirit of his religion in action on an international scale, is of great importance. For the time has come when the world feels that religion cannot remain foreign to burning questions of international interest such as that of war. No teaching which ignores those questions can therefore really appeal to modern consciousness.

If God and Caesar are in conflict with each other, then they cannot both claim our allegiance. If we do not deify the nation and sacrifice God, renouncing all values beyond the national ones, then we must consider the problem of war and conquest in the light of the highest religious values and, if necessary, sacrifice the interest of the nation. No great Western teacher has done so, save Akhenaten. None could do so, for none had the power to make peace and war. And the few among our modern pacifists who boast of doing so now, put forward their claims from an armchair, for none of them has any say in the decisions of his country's government.

If, by taking the unusual course which he did, Akhenaten lost an empire, he at least left the world an example forever which was worth its while. In all simplicity, without theorizing on right and wrong, he showed us in what direction is to be sought the solution of the war problem, if one does not want to sacrifice truth to the state.

RETURN OF THE PRINCE OF PEACE

In January 1907, a skeleton—all that remained of the world's first rationalist and oldest Prince of Peace—was discovered by Weigall and Ayrton in a tomb in the royal necropolis near the ruins of Thebes.[2] At the foot of the coffin was inscribed the prayer, previously quoted, most probably composed by the dead king himself, in praise of the one God for the sake of whom he had lost everything.

On the top of the coffin were the name and titles of the Pharaoh:

> "The beautiful Prince, the Chosen-son of the Sun, King of Upper and Lower Egypt, Living in Truth, Lord of the Two Lands. Akhenaten, the beautiful Child of the living Aten, whose name shall live for ever and ever."

The name had been erased, but the titles were sufficient to reconstruct the inscription in its whole.

The tomb had once been that of Akhenaten's mother. The body of the young Pharaoh had been brought there from Akhet-aten, after the desertion of the sacred city by the Egyptian court, under Tutankhamen, and laid next to the remains of the deceased queen. But soon after, the priests of Amun, restored to power, had found it proper to remove Queen Tiye's mummy to another place. Akhenaten's body, wrapped in its double sheets of pure gold, had been left alone in the sepulcher. Century after century it had remained there, forgotten. And as the priests had not cared to seal the entrance of the lonely chamber properly, the dampness of the air had penetrated it and had slowly caused the embalmed flesh to decay. So that, after 3,300 years, when human eyes once more beheld the young king who had sung the glory of life, nothing was left of his mortal form but dry bones.

The discovery was a subject of discussion among scholars for some time. Apart from that, it remained unnoticed. After examining the skeleton, Professor Elliot Smith declared that the Pharaoh could not have been more than 28 or 29 when he died. Arthur Weigall, a few years later, published his beautiful book, *The Life and Times of Akhnaton*, in which he asserts himself as a genuine admirer of the Pharaoh and of his teaching.

---

[2] [See Preface for a discussion of this discovery. –ed.]

But no such interest as was roused, in 1922, by Lord Carnarvon's discovery of the tomb of Tutankhamen, was stirred among the public at large. There were no articles written for lay people in the Sunday editions of the daily papers about the most perfect man whom the Western world had produced. No romantic history for popular consumption came forth overnight. No lectures were given in literary and semi-literary circles. No tea-table talk took place around the Pharaoh's name. For little had been found of those treasures which impress the imagination of crowds: no jewels; no gems; no gilded furniture; nothing but the skeleton of a god-like man who had died, rejected and cursed 3,300 years before.

Yet that man was the one the world had been unconsciously seeking all the time, through centuries of moral unrest, disillusionment, and failure.

EVEN IN DARKNESS, ALL IS LIGHT

Confident in their suddenly re-acquired power, and maddened by the joy of revenge, the priests of Amun had decided to wipe out every trace of Akhenaten's memory forever. The temples of the various gods were restored and their cult reinstalled in all its former splendor. And a curse was proclaimed throughout the land against him who had dared to forsake the traditional path and preach the way of the one God.

Let us remember the hour of his defeat. Let us think of the national cult. Let us picture to ourselves the huge affluence of pilgrims from all parts of the empire, assembled there to see the old order begin again. They came to hear the old prayers and the old songs in honor of the god of Thebes—of the god of Egypt—who had made Egypt great, and who would have helped her to remain so, had it not been for the "apostate" king, who had risen against him. Let us imagine the smoke and fragrance of incense, the music of the holy instruments amplified through the successive halls of granite. Picture the flame of the sacrifice, reflected upon the dusky faces, and upon the golden hieroglyphics shining in the darkness in praise of Amun, king of gods.

And in the midst of all this, echoing from hall to hall, telling the world of that day and the world to come that the "criminal of Akhet-aten" had been vanquished, and that Egypt was herself once more, the song of triumph and of hate:

> "Woe to him who assails thee, O Amun!
> Thy city endures,
> but he who assailed thee falls."

...the song of the victorious crowd led by its cunning shepherds over the dead body of Him who, being one with the Sun, walked in His own light. In short, of the divine individual:

> "The abode of him who assailed thee is in darkness,
> but the rest of the earth is in light..."

In that crowd from all parts of the empire, there were men who had known King Akhenaten in the days of his glory. They were men who had received from him gifts in gold and silver, and to whom he had spoken kind words, and on whom he had relied, believing them to be faithful. But not one of them stirred as he heard the frenzied hymn of hate. The priests of Amun got what they wanted. The world obeyed them—not Him. And it has continued obeying them ever since, cherishing its manifold superstitions and paying homage to its tribal gods. To the present day, no man has yet raised his voice and openly challenged their triumph in the name of the Child of Light whom they persecuted beyond death.

But there is one thing that the priests could *not* do. They could not keep the world from groping in search of the dream—or the reality—for which he had lived. They could not stop the evolution of the spirit, nor put an end to the quest of truth.

While Akhenaten's memory was rapidly being effaced, the quasi-universality of Sun-worship was a fact. However wanting were the different conceptions of the Sun held in different countries, still it was to the fiery Disk that all men rendered praise, in some way or the other, justifying the words of the inspired king. And no force on earth could keep that unanimity from meaning what it did.

As time passed, the better men of the Western world began to feel the limitations of their man-made religions. They craved a faith that should be founded solely upon the facts of existence. They sought a faith that should include the whole scheme of life, and not man alone, within its scope. They longed for a faith that should also find its practical application in questions of international interest no less than in the private behavior of individuals. And at the same time, a faith that should be simple, extremely simple—the world is tired of intricate metaphysics, of sterile mental play centered around ideas that correspond to nothing important in living life. In other words, as one imperfect creed after another rose, thrived, and decayed in its turn, leaving behind it disillusionment and doubt and moral sickness, the better men have been unknowingly seeking for the lost truth preached by King Akhenaten.

Deprived of name and fame and of the love of men, the royal youth lay in the desecrated tomb in which his enemies had put his body, while centuries rolled on. And no one knew that the light that the best ones were still seeking was his light. The discovery of his bones was no more noticed than any other archaeological discovery. In all appearance, his persecutors still held their sway. But they could not silence the yearning of Western consciousness for a truly rational religion in tune with life, uniting the scientific spirit to all-embracing love.

The discovery of Akhenaten's remains was hardly spoken of, save in very restricted scholarly circles. But times were already beginning to ripen for the recognition of his teaching as the gospel of a new and better world—for his long-delayed triumph. Petrie had already proclaimed the eternal actuality of the Religion of the Disk in the early 1890s. Perhaps now, finally, Akhenaten's time has come. I believe that no faith could respond to the demands of the modern world better than Akhenaten's worship of cosmic energy, the essence of life, through the beautiful Disk of our parent star in which it radiates as light and heat.

After killing the Religion of the Disk and thrusting their country back into the path that was to lead it to slow decay, the priests of Egypt believed that Akhenaten and his teaching were dead forever. They were sure no man would ever rise in favor of him whom they had condemned, and they departed content from the great temple where his doom had been solemnized. And we have seen that, for 3,300 years, their unholy verdict held good. One can think of no other historic instance of hatred being successful for such a long time.

But the hour has come for the age-old injustice to end. It is the duty of the modern man to challenge the judgment of the priests of the outdated local deity, and to undo what they have done; to answer their hymn of hate; to proclaim the glory of the most lovable of men; to teach the children that are growing up to hold his name sacred; to look up to him as to their own beloved King. And above all, to live in accordance with his teaching of life.

May we consider that duty also as a privilege—perhaps the greatest privilege of our troubled times—and may we feel proud to accomplish it without failure. And then, even as the Sun reappears in the East after a long night, Akhenaten shall rise again from the dust of dead history, in youth and beauty, and live in the consciousness of our times and of all times to come, and rule the hearts and lives of the elite of the world, "till the swan shall turn black and the crow turn white, till the hills rise up to travel and the deeps rush into the rivers."

Fig. 13: Akhenaten and Nefertiti.

SHORTER HYMN TO ATEN

(AFTER LICHTHEIM)

Adoration of *Re-Horakhty-who-rejoices-in-the-Two-Horizons,* in his name, *Shu-who-is-in-the-Aten*, who gives life forever, by the King who lives by Maat, the Lord of the Two Lands: *Neferkheprure, Sole-one-of-Re*; the Son of Re who lives by Maat, the Lord of crowns: *Akhenaten*, great in his lifetime, given life forever.

(1)
Splendid you rise, O living Aten, eternal lord!
You are radiant, beauteous, mighty,
Your love is great, immense.
Your rays light up all faces,
Your bright hue gives life to hearts,
When you fill the Two Lands with your love.
August God who fashioned himself,
Who made every land, created what is in it,
All peoples, herds, and flocks,
All trees that grow from soil;
They live when you dawn for them,
You are mother and father of all that you made.

(2)
When you dawn their eyes observe you,
As your rays light the whole earth;
Every heart acclaims your sight,
When you are risen as their lord.
When you set in sky's western horizon of heaven,
They lie down as if to die,
Their heads covered, their noses stopped,
Until you dawn in sky's eastern horizon of heaven.
Their arms adore your soul,
As you nourish the hearts by your beauty;
One lives when you cast your rays,
Every land is in festivity.

(3)

Singers, musicians, shout with joy,
In the court of the Benben-shrine,
And in all temples in Akhet-aten,
The place of truth in which you rejoice.
Foods are offered in their midst,
Your holy son performs your praises,
O Aten living in his risings,
And all your creatures leap before you.
Your august son exults in joy,
O Aten living daily content in the sky,
Your offspring, your august son, Sole one of Re;
The Son of Re does not cease to extol his beauty,
Neferkheprure, Sole-one-of Re.

(4)

I am your son who serves you, who exalts your name,
Your power, your strength, are firm in my heart;
You are the living Aten whose image endures,
You have made the far sky to shine in it,
To observe all that you made.
You are One yet a million lives are in you,
To make them live, you give the breath of life to their noses;
By the sight of your rays all flowers exist,
What lives and sprouts from the soil grows when you shine.
Drinking deep of your sight all flocks frisk,
The birds in the nest fly up in joy;
Their folded wings unfold in praise
Of the living Aten, their maker.

LONGER HYMN TO ATEN

(AFTER PRITCHARD)

(1)

Thou risest beautiful upon the horizon of heaven,
Thou living Aten, the beginning of life!
When thou art risen on the eastern horizon,
Thou hast filled every land with thy beauty.
Thou art gracious, great, glistening, and high over every land;
Thy rays encompass the lands to the limit of all that thou hast made:

As thou art Re, thou reachest to the end of them;
Thou subduest them for thy beloved son.
Thou art far away, yet thy rays are on earth;
Thou art plainly visible, yet no one knows thy going.

(2)

When thou settest in the western horizon,
The land is in darkness, in the manner of death.
They sleep in a room, with heads wrapped up,
Nor sees one eye the other.
All their goods which are under their heads might be stolen,
But they would not perceive it.
Every lion is come forth from his den;
All creeping things, they sting.
Darkness is a shroud, and the earth is in stillness,
For he who made them rests in his horizon.

(3)

At daybreak, when thou arisest on the horizon,
When thou shinest as the Aten by day,
Thou drivest away the darkness and givest thy rays.
The Two Lands are in festivity every day,
Awake and standing upon their feet,
For thou hast raised them up.
Washing their bodies, taking their clothing,
Their arms are raised in praise at thy appearance.
All the world, they do their work.

(4)

All beasts are content in the fields;
Trees and plants are flourishing.
The birds which fly from their nests,
Their wings are stretched out in praise to thy soul.
All beasts spring upon their feet.
Whatever flies and alights,
They live when thou hast risen for them.
The ships are sailing north and south as well,
For every way is open at thy appearance.
The fish in the river dart before thy face;
Thy rays are in the midst of the great green sea.

(5)

Creator of seed in women,
Thou who makest fluid into man,
Who maintainest the son in the womb of his mother,
Who soothest him with that which stills his weeping,
Thou nurse even in the womb,
Who givest breath to sustain all that he has made!
When he descends from the womb to breathe
On the day when he is born,
Thou openest his mouth completely,
Thou suppliest his necessities.

(6)

When the chick in the egg speaks within the shell,
Thou givest him breath within it to maintain him.
When thou hast made him his fulfillment within the egg, to break it,
He comes forth from the egg to speak at his completed time;
He walks upon his legs when he comes forth from it.

(7)
How manifold it is, what thou hast made!
They are hidden from the face of man.
O sole god, like whom there is no other!
Thou didst create the world according to thy desire,
Whilst thou wert alone: All men, cattle, and wild beasts,
Whatever is on earth, going upon its feet,
And what is on high, flying with its wings.

(8)
The countries of Syria, Nubia, and the land of Egypt,
Thou settest every man in his place,
Thou suppliest their needs:
Everyone has his food, and his time of life is reckoned.
Their tongues are separate in speech,
And their natures as well;
Their skins are distinguished,
As thou distinguishest the foreign peoples.

(9)
Thou makest a Nile in the underworld,
Thou bringest forth as thou desirest
To maintain the people of Egypt
According as thou madest them for thyself,
The lord of all of them, wearying himself with them,
The lord of every land, rising for them,
The Aten of the day, great of majesty.

All distant foreign countries, thou makest their life also,
For thou hast set a Nile in heaven,
That it may descend for them and make waves upon the mountains,
Like the great green sea,
To water their fields in their towns.

(10)
How effective they are, thy plans, O lord of eternity!
The Nile in heaven, it is for the foreign peoples
And for the beasts of every desert that go upon their feet;
While the true Nile comes from the underworld for Egypt.

Thy rays suckle every meadow.
When thou risest, they live, they grow for thee.
Thou makest the seasons in order to rear all that thou hast made,
The winter to cool them,
And the heat that they may taste thee.
Thou hast made the distant sky in order to rise therein,
In order to see all that thou dost make.

(11)
Whilst thou wert alone,
Rising in thy form as the living Aten,
Appearing, shining, withdrawing or approaching,
Thou madest millions of forms of thyself alone.
Cities, towns, fields, road, and river —
Every eye beholds thee over against them,
For thou art the Aten of the day over the earth.

(12)
Thou art in my heart,
And there is no other that knows thee
Save thy son Akhenaten,
For thou hast made him well-versed in thy plans and in thy strength.

The world came into being by thy hand,
According as thou hast made it.
When thou hast risen, it lives,
When thou settest, it dies.
Thou art lifetime thy own self,
For one lives only through thee.
Eyes are fixed on beauty until thou settest.
All work is laid aside when thou settest in the west.
But when thou risest again,
Everything is made to flourish for the king,
Since thou didst found the earth
And raise them up for thy son,
Who came forth from thy body.

(Closing)
The King of Upper and Lower Egypt, Akhenaten,
And the Chief Wife of the King, Nefertiti,
Living and youthful forever and ever.

Fig. 14: Akhenaten and Nefertiti make an offering to the Aten.

EPILOGUE: FROM LIGHT TO LIGHT

DAVID SKRBINA

We read in the Bible, "From dust we have come, and to dust we shall return" (Gen 3:19). What a degrading vision of humanity!—though perhaps appropriate for a book that dwells on the evils of earthly existence. Even granting that we are, in a crude sense, "dust," this dust was forged in the hearts of long-distant stars. Stars live by creating two intimately connected things: *light* and *matter*. These two substances comprise the material structure of the known universe—the very cosmos of which are a part. Thus it is unsurprising that our greatest scientists have determined that 'matter is energy (light)' and 'energy is matter.' In essence, they accept the view that *all is light*. Without even realizing it, they are rearticulating ancient wisdom.

Were the writer of the above biblical passage truly inspired by the divine, he would have written, "From light we have come, and to light we shall return."

Since the time of Akhenaten, various philosophers and thinkers have sensed the importance of the Light. It is perhaps no coincidence that the God of the Old Testament begins his creation by proclaiming, "Let there be light," and that his erstwhile son, the savior of mankind, declared himself "the light of the world." For Plato, the light of the sun was the ideal metaphor for his highest of forms—the Good. In post-Aristotelian Greece, the Stoic philosophers envisioned the cosmos as heading toward a state that they called *ekpyrosis*—pure, bright, incandescent light. Circa 1200 AD, British philosopher Robert Grosseteste developed a comprehensive worldview based on the metaphysics of light. Francisco Patrizi's *New Philosophy of the Universe* (1585) dedicated an entire section to "*Panaugia*" or the All-Light.

With the scientific developments of the late 1800s, however, light became degraded into mere physical quantities: photons, waves, fields, and so on. Light was just one more form of energy, and it was stripped of any metaphysical or philosophical significance. Today light is: fluorescent tubes, neon signs, laser beams, and the ominous blue glow that emanates from our favorite iDevice. Light has become quantified, dissected, commodified, and debased. Not coincidentally, so too has our vision of humanity and the universe.

Conventional science seems to be reaching the limit of its ability to comprehend the nature of light—not to mention the Big Light from which all has arisen. When astrophysicists contemplate the origins of the Big Bang, they are left gasping for answers. Some suggest that it arose "from nothing," perhaps as a kind of fluctuation in the quantum vacuum. But both their own theories of conservation, and ancient wisdom, suggest that this is impossible. The notion of the universe arising from nothing more likely suggests that the horizon of scientific knowledge has been reached. This thought gets further confirmation from the new concepts of 'dark matter' and 'dark energy,' of which scientists can say almost nothing and yet, on their own account, comprise something like 96% of the cosmos. Hence it is clear: The Something from which all arises is in the realm of metaphysics, and thus amenable to philosophic inquiry alone.

Among current philosophers, perhaps only Henryk Skolimowski has taken the philosophy of light to heart. Long a subtext of his writings, the topic became explicit in his 2010 book *Let There be Light*. Drawing inspiration from both East and West, Skolimowski outlines an ethical and metaphysical system that surely would have brought a smile to Akhenaten's face. A few others have dabbled in the philosophy of light—such as physicist Manoj Thulasidas' book *The Unreal Universe* (2007). But apart from these rare exceptions, contemporary thinkers have yet to engage in anything like a true philosophy of light.

We await future philosophers to carry on this task. We can envision a new metaphysics of light. Akhenaten has shown us the way. We need only resurrect his spirit, his courage, and his vision.

BIBLIOGRAPHY

Aldred, C. 1968. *Akhenaten Pharaoh of Egypt*. McGraw-Hill.

Aldred, C. 1973. *Akhenaten and Nefertity*. Viking.

Aldred, C. 1988. *Akhenaten: King of Egypt*. Thames and Hudson.

Assmann, J. 1997. *Moses the Egyptian*. Harvard University Press.

Baikie, J. 1926. *The Amarna Age*. Macmillan.

Breasted, J. 1906. *Ancient Records of Egypt*. University of Chicago Press.

Breasted, J. 1910. *A History of the Ancient Egyptians*. C. Scribner's Sons.

Breasted, J. 1912. *A History of Egypt*. C. Scribner's Sons.

Budge, W. 1923/1989. *Tutankamun, Amenism, Atenism, and Egyptian Monotheism*. Ayer.

Davies, N. 1903-08. *The Rock-Tombs of el-Amarna*. Egyptian Exploration Fund.

Hall, H. 1936. *The Ancient History of the Near East*. Methuen.

Hawass, Z. et al. 2010. "Ancestry and pathology in King Tutankhamun's family." *JAMA* (17 Feb.).

Hornung, E. 1995. *Akhenaten and the Religion of Light*. Cornell University Press.

Lichtheim, M. 1973. *Ancient Egyptian Literature* (vol. 2). University of California Press.

Matthews, V. and Benjamin, D. 2006. *Old Testament Parallels*. Paulist Press.

Montserrat, D. 2000. *Akhenaten*. Routledge.

Peet, T. 1923. *The City of Akhenaten*. Egyptian Exploration Fund.

Pendlebury, J. 1935. *Tell el-Amarna*. Dickson and Thompson.

Petrie, F. 1894. *Tell el-Amarna*. Methuen.

Petrie, F. 1904. *A History of Egypt*. Methuen.

Petrie, F. 1924. *Religious Life in Ancient Egypt*. Houghton Mifflin.

Redford, D. 1984. *Akhenaten: The Heretic King*. Princeton University Press.

Redford, D. 1987. "The monotheism of the heretic pharaoh." *Biblical Archaeology Review* 13(3).

Samson, J. 1972. *Amarna, City of Akhenaten and Nefertiti*. Aris and Phillips.

Skolimowski, H. 2010. *Let There Be Light*. New Delhi: Wisdom Tree.

Thulasidas, M. 2007. *The Unreal Universe*. Asian Books.

Weigall, A. 1922. *The Life and Times of Akhnaton*. Butterworth.

Weigall, A. 1923. *Tutankhamen and Other Essays*. Butterworth.

Weigall, A. 1934. *A Short History of Ancient Egypt*. Chapman and Hall.

INDEX

194

Made in the USA
Las Vegas, NV
09 May 2021

22730007R00108

ALSO BY FRANKLYN M. BRANLEY

MYSTERIES OF THE UNIVERSE SERIES
Mysteries of Outer Space
Mysteries of the Satellites
Mysteries of the Universe

Black Holes, White Dwarfs, and Superstars
Columbia & Beyond
    The Story of the Space Shuttle
Comets, Meteoroids, and Asteroids
    Mavericks of the Solar System
The Earth: *Planet Number Three*
The Electromagnetic Spectrum
    Key to the Universe
Halley: Comet 1986
Jupiter
    King of the Gods, Giant of the Planets
Mars: *Planet Number Four*
The Milky Way: *Galaxy Number One*
The Moon: *Earth's Natural Satellite*
The Nine Planets
Space Colony
    Frontier of the 21st Century
The Sun: *Star Number One*